Reinventing Church

STORIES OF HOPE *from* FOUR ANGLICAN PARISHES

JAMES COLLINS, HELEN COLLINS *and* DOUGLAS EZZY

WIPF & STOCK · Eugene, Oregon

Wipf and Stock Publishers
199 W 8th Ave, Suite 3
Eugene, OR 97401

Reinventing Church
Stories of Hope from Four Anglican Parishes
By Collins, James and Collins, Helen

ISBN 13: 978-1-5326-0625-0
Publication date 8/11/2016
Previously published by Morning Star Publishing, 2016

Acknowledgements

This book would not have been possible without the participation of many people from the four rural Anglican communities of faith (New Norfolk, Channel/Cygnet, St Helens, and Hamilton). We thank them all for giving so freely of themselves.

We are grateful for the advice of Gary Easthope, Gary Bouma, and Douglas Pratt. They read various drafts and offered constructive advice on how to improve it. We are very thankful for the assistance of Della Clark, Lyn Devereaux, Andrea Michaelson, and Denise Jones for their administrative support and friendship over many years.

Contents

Introduction

This book tells the stories of four rural Anglican communities of faith in Tasmania who have adopted Enabler Supported Ministry (ESM). We tell a story of hope against a background of decline in rural communities and rural parishes. It is a story of how people in these four parishes adopted a different model for parish communities (ESM) and a future for their parishes, which included care for their wider communities.

Stories provide direction, security, meaning, purpose, and hope. Stories "bind us together" (Staudenmaier 1988: 314). These characteristics are revealed in the stories of the four parishes in this book. Through telling new stories parishioners found hope, direction, and security in a new future. They discovered new meaning and purpose in the renewal of life in their parishes and in their connection to the wider community.

In any situation, 'change' can be hard to cope with, and parish life is no different. Often the response to change is to try to resist it, to cling to what we know, and to how things have always been done. In a rapidly changing world that is increasingly secular and pluralistic, the Church's reaction is typically one of "*resistance to change*" (Dowie 1997: 147, italics in original). This response can also be characterized by deference and subordination to authority, dissonance within the congregational culture, dependency, and decline (Dowie 1997).

Stories help us understand 'change'. This study demonstrates that acceptance of change can be a life-affirming experience. In the parishes described in this book, the acceptance of change facilitated growth and connectedness. These four communities of faith took a direction that many in the hierarchy of the Church resist because it is not the same as traditional structures within the Church and that many parishioners resist because difference is inherently frightening and unsettling.

There are very few books about the practices and stories of contemporary mainstream Christianity, particularly in rural locations (Frankenberg 1969) and most particularly in Australia. Most academic studies are large-scale statistical analyses which tend to be focussed on church attendance and identification. In the United States, there are rare exceptions to this, such as Warner (1990) and Ammerman (1990, 1994, 2001), but these studies are typically urban, not rural. In Australia, Hughes and Kunciunas (2009) have recently completed a study of models of leadership and organization in Anglican churches in rural Australia.

This book is based on thirty interviews with various people in four parishes. These people are typical of the cross-section of 'locals' in each community. That is, some are long-term residents having lived in the towns and/or districts for over thirty years. Others had moved to the towns and/ or districts more recently because of the life-style and/or attractive scenery and weather. The interviews were all conducted by Rev. James Collins. The interviewees included people with whom Rev. Collins has worked closely and who supported ESM from the beginning. Other people interviewed were, initially, antagonistic to the idea of ESM and the changes it would bring to the parishes. Without exception, all such people became supportive of ESM as it was introduced and practiced as a model of being church in all four parishes. Rev. James Collins was the 'Enabler' of the parishes described in this book from mid-2001 until early 2007.

There are four main changes associated with the introduction of Enabler supported ministry. First, ESM shapes the operation of power within the parishes. There has been a marked democratization in the decision making process. This has resulted in a broader level of participation across the whole parish by the parishioners, and also by the wider community as each of the parishes has actively sought to engage with their local communities. In other words, there has been a change from one person, the priest, exercising enormous power within the parish to that power being dispersed throughout the whole parish and, indeed, shared with the wider community.

Second, ESM changes gender dynamics. There has been a significant re-orientation from a male dominated environment within the parishes where men held most, if not all, of the positions of power to a situation where power is shared equally by all, regardless of age and gender. Women now participate fully in all aspects of the life of the parishes and have a voice at all levels of decision making.

Third, ESM changes organizational structure. The parishes have moved from a 'wagon wheel' model to a 'spider's web' model. In the former model, where the priest is at the centre and the spokes represent the parishioners, all attention is focused on the priest as the centre of parish life and activities, whereas in the latter model, there is a far more organic inter-connectedness between the parishioners and, along with them, the members of the wider community.

Fourth, ESM has refocused the central concerns of each of the parishes onto church life and community engagement. Previously the parishes were primarily focused on finances. These financial concerns involved raising enough money to afford a full-time stipendiary priest along with meeting all of the diocesan requirements of annual assessment (the diocesan 'tax'). Now the primary concerns of each of the parishes are focused more on the well-being of all parishioners (including the on-going provision of sacramental worship and pastoral care) and engagement with the community. Ammerman (2001) considers that this capacity to hold together the particular, the local context, with the universal, the wider society, gives communities of faith the resilience they require for a sustainable future. As a consequence of the introduction of ESM these four parishes are now robust and resilient enough to be able to engage with on-going change.

Becoming Enabler Supported Ministry parishes has fundamentally changed these parishes. There is a more equitable distribution of power, greater gender equality, a more organic structure, and their primary concerns are parishioner well-being and engagement with the wider community. Parishes with Enabler Supported Ministry tend to focus outward and engage with the wider community. This is in contrast to the former structures within the parishes where the primary focus was inward and was concerned with maintaining the existing power structures within each parish. Due to these changes, the parishes have been able to welcome and incorporate newcomers and they, too, have now come to participate fully in the life of the parish. Ammerman (2001) maintains that this capacity to incorporate new members into a community of faith is crucial for its well-being.

The remainder of this Introduction provides a short description of the development of Enabler Supported Ministry in Tasmania. We then describe the four main dimensions of our theoretical approach to the study of Anglicanism in rural contexts: rural decline, secularization and pluralism, postmodernism, and cultural framing.

Enabler Supported Ministry in the Diocese of Tasmania

The Diocese of Tasmania was in a state of serious decline in the late 1990's. The impressions of the Diocese from the then Diocesan Ministry Officer are worth quoting at length as they provide an insightful account of the Diocese at the beginning of ESM in Tasmania:

> When I arrived in Tasmania the situation seemed to me to be very fraught. The economic decline in rural and more isolated areas was severe and there were serious systemic problems in the church. These communities had been hammered by the shift in the whole economic landscape. People were moving out and businesses and services were closing which was proving very painful. At the same time, within the Anglican Church, there was the unfolding story of clergy abuse and misuse of power, which was having a significant impact on church and clergy morale.
>
> I think the *Moving Out – Moving On* report [see below] provided momentum towards something rather different in terms of how the Diocese might go about resourcing churches in those places that were hurting most. This resonated strongly with my own experiences of urban ministry in poor communities in the UK. I felt that I could make a contribution from those experiences, particularly my work with churches that wanted to stand in greater solidarity with the people in their communities suffering as a consequence of globalisation. (Claude, priest)[1]

Not only were rural parishes in Tasmania suffering badly from declining numbers and falling income, they were also affected by the financial model operating in Australian dioceses. In England, diocesan money is pooled and re-distributed to maintain poorer parishes, whereas in Australia, "churches either sink or swim according to the money they can raise themselves" (Claude, priest). Early on in his work in Tasmania, Claude realized that the combination of factors such as financial viability of parishes and the pitfalls of amalgamation were creating serious problems:

> The rural communities in Tasmania were clearly suffering from declining congregations and income. Resources and people were draining out of communities and, at the same time, churches were trying to find ways of raising a full annual stipend and everything that goes with maintaining a clergy person in residence and this was proving unsustainable. The way in which the Diocese had

1 The names of all interviewees referred to in quotations taken from the interview transcriptions are pseudonyms; this is a requirement of the University Ethics Committee.

> tried to address this prior to the *Moving Out – Moving On* report was to amalgamate parishes and clearly that had not worked. You ended up with either amalgamation or closure or amalgamation and then closure.
>
> Amalgamation of parishes was also having a debilitating effect on clergy ... [who] were ... racing across the countryside from church to church trying to fulfil all the demands expected of them as deliverers of ministry to and for the people. This unhealthy and unsustainable way of being church urgently needed to be addressed and it was clear the solution would need to be much more than a patch-up job.
> (Claude, priest)

Claude's insights and observations concur with Rev James Collins' assessment and experience of working in the Diocese of Tasmania, and these are confirmed by statistical data about Tasmania and the Anglican Church. Recognizing the crucial relationship between social and cultural change and the state of parishes, particularly rural parishes, in Tasmania, is a necessary precursor to understanding the current state of the Diocese and the options available to address the continuing problem of parish decline.

This decline throughout rural Tasmania is also highlighted in the findings of the report, *Dropping off the Edge: the distribution of disadvantage in Australia*, by Professor Tony Vinson (2007). This report found that in Tasmania just four of the State's 29 Local Government Areas account for 43.3 percent of the top ranked positions of the key indicators of disadvantage. On the list of Tasmania's most disadvantaged municipalities were Break O'Day (where St Helens Parish is located), Central Highlands (where Hamilton Parish is located), and Derwent Valley (where New Norfolk Parish is located). All these parishes have adopted Enabler Supported Ministry (ESM) as a way of being church. The report, *Dropping off the Edge* (Vinson 2007), found that the major characteristics of these municipalities include low family income; higher rates of disability, sickness, mortality, and suicide; higher rates of criminal convictions and prison admissions; higher rates of unemployment and long-term unemployment; and also limited computer use and internet access.

The 'unsettled times' (Ammerman 2001) experienced by the rural (and many urban) parishes in Tasmania led to a review of the viability of all parishes in the Diocese of Tasmania. In 1996, during the episcopacy of Bishop Phillip

Newell, the Synod of the Diocese of Tasmania received the final report from the Viability and Restructuring Committee entitled *Moving Out – Moving On* (Anglican Church of Australia, Diocese of Tasmania 1996). During Bishop Newell's episcopacy the recommendations of this report were implemented, and in 2002 the synodical legislation was enacted by the Diocese to legislate for the place of ESM within the Diocese and for the role of the Enabler within ESM parishes (see Appendix 4). The *Moving Out – Moving On* report (Anglican Church of Australia, Diocese of Tasmania) 1996: 5) made some insightful observations, including the following:

1. "new models for ministry are required";
2. the "present model of ministry has been identified as static, directed towards itself, and bound to territory";
3. there is "an atmosphere of defensiveness and clergy centredness"; and
4. the diversity of the Church, "demographically, sociologically, theologically, and liturgically means that no one model will be appropriate for every parish or ministry".

The Report also had several significant implications for the life of the Diocese:

1. the Synod in 1996 made the decision not to replace the, then, Assistant (or Suffragan) Bishop as episcopal ministry was perceived to be a hindrance to the development of new ways of being church;
2. it was recommended that the Diocese appoint a Diocesan Ministry Officer to walk alongside parishes developing new approaches in the life and mission of the church and to develop collegiality at the grass-roots level. A priest was appointed as the Diocesan Ministry Officer in 1998; and
3. it was recommended that team ministries be developed between clergy and laity to lead parishes.

ESM as it is implemented in Tasmania resonates with ideas across the Anglican Church world-wide. It is noteworthy that some of the poorest rural areas in Tasmania have been instrumental in developing this new model of Anglican ministry. Such ministry "'taps into the depth of talent and leadership in the local community'" (Briggs 2002: 5, quoting Harrower). In Enabler Supported Ministry (ESM), people from local Anglican communities of faith have been ordained without formal theological education to minister locally alongside other lay leaders also 'called' (that is, chosen by the parish) to specific ministries within the Local Ministry Support Team (LMST).

In the introduction and implementation of ESM in the Anglican Diocese of Tasmania, under Bishop Newell (and later ratified under Bishop Harrower), the Diocesan Ministry Officer drew on concepts of mission based on the missiology of Roland Allen. As Bishop Harrower (2009: 207) explains, this was foundational to the Diocese's establishment of

> a pattern of parish life known as Enabler Supported Ministry. Parishes who could no longer afford reasonable levels of stipendiary ministry, yet sustained a heart for ministry and mission in their districts, would be enabled to continue in full ministry. The priority was to sustain the mission of the church rather than institutional guidelines or inherited structures.

Bishop Harrower (2004: 13) sees the development of teams in Tasmania "with the assistance of enablers … giving leadership to congregational life throughout the state" as being one of the main elements of creating a healthy church in Tasmania. Bishop Harrower (2004: 16) goes on to say that he is

> fully convinced that the concept of "Enabler Supported Ministry" leadership is a key ministry model for us. Releasing local people to mission and ministry requires the training of a team of skilled and competent enablers. Those who serve in this capacity must have access to all the resources necessary to fulfil their responsibilities.

Enabler Supported Ministry (ESM) is a model of church where local people are called to form a leadership team known as the Local Ministry Support Team (LMST). The LMST, supported by the Enabler, takes on the responsibility for carrying forward the ministry and mission of the parish, along with the whole community of faith. Jane and Graham, who have both been members of the LMST in their respective parishes for over nine years, describe ESM in the following ways:

> Enabler Supported Ministry is a ministry which encourages participation … by all parishioners or as many as possible. It encourages people to discover and use their gifts within the church. It probably does away with the traditional hierarchy in that all gifts are acknowledged as being equally valuable and some people aren't valued more than others. Of course, it is supported by an Enabler

> who is a person who isn't a parishioner, but a person who has the necessary experience, qualifications and personality to act as an Enabler within the parish and also to be a link between the parish and the Diocese. (Jane, artist)
>
> I believe it's an accountable form of ministry where the Anglican Church and Anglican ethos can be worked out at a local level with the sacramental ministries being attended to and the pastoral ministries being attended to. So it's a very broad range of ministry that is structured; [it] doesn't just happen in an ad hoc manner. (Graham, business proprietor)

This book tells the stories of four rural Anglican communities of faith in Tasmania. In this telling, we demonstrate how the theological conceptual framework of ESM both facilitated and encouraged these parishes to engage with their context and to care not only for each other but also for those in the wider community. We draw on a number of theorists, such as Berger, Lyon, and Bouma, whose work crosses the boundaries between sociology and theology. This ethnography is grounded in a sociological framework that not only takes heed of the social and cultural context but that also recognizes the centrality of theology to these communities of faith. These parishes honestly faced the consequences of their long-standing decline and through ESM created a new future for themselves and a new capacity to engage with their local communities. To their surprise, they found that, indeed, ESM resulted in growth and hope.

The increasing demise, both numerically and financially, of so many parishes across Tasmania, and Australia generally, is a pressing problem for the Anglican Church. It is also an acute problem for many churches in the Western world, and not only Anglican. This story, then, is worth telling not only because it is a story of hope about four rural Anglican Tasmanian parishes but also because it clearly demonstrates that the adoption of a different way of being church (ESM), which is informed by a grounding in sociologically informed theology, can reverse what appears to be inevitable decline. To recognize the gravity of one's situation and to make the decision to change is a brave act of stepping out into the unknown with no guarantees. It takes courage. And this courage is fuelled by hope, even if it is only "'a shy hope in the heart'" (Thornhill 1992: 172-173 cited by Bouma 2006: 2).

Having said this, though, ESM will not be suitable for or applicable in all parishes. There are some parishes that might have been able to make the transition to ESM a decade ago but, because of the inexorable loss of people from the district and the Parish, they are now unable to form an ESM Local Ministry Support Team. There are also other parishes that might have been well suited to adopting ESM because of the changing nature of their social and cultural context but their understanding of the nature of leadership in the church precluded them from accepting a model of shared leadership. In these situations despite not being able to afford a full-time stipendiary priest, they still wanted this to occur. That is, their conceptual framework (theology/ church culture) prevents them from making a response to the changing nature of their social and cultural context. Further to this, many parishes are unable to become ESM parishes as they have experienced major conflict in their recent history and this has left them diminished in energy and unable to make any positive decisions about their future.

Contemporary Anglicanism in Rural Contexts

Four significant works on the Anglican Church in Australia contain scant reference to the issues facing rural parishes. In *Anglicanism in Australia: A History* (2002) there are only a few references made to the rural situation. For instance, Hilliard (2002: 144), in the chapter he contributed to this book, makes the point that

> One by one during the 1990's rural dioceses grappled with what was freely admitted to be a crisis and pondered new ways of providing ministry in large regions which could no longer maintain full-time paid clergy. Almost everyone agreed that for both theological and practical reasons pastoral leadership should in future be based in the local congregation. In Tasmania, for example, more than half of the fifty-eight parishes were deemed financially unviable in 1995. The diocese then launched an ambitious scheme of restructuring.

There are three other significant works on the Anglican Church in Australia by Frame (2007), Carnley (2004), and Hale and Curnow (2009). In *Anglicans in Australia*, Frame (2007) makes no real reference to the rural situation facing many parishes and, indeed, many dioceses in Australia. Carnley (2004) does not address this situation either in his book, *Reflections in Glass* (2004), although he does make a fleeting reference to total and collaborative ministry but his main emphasis remains on traditional models of priestly ministry. Brain (2009), in a recent work edited by Hale and Curnow entitled *Facing the Future: Bishops Imagine a Different Church*, contributes a chapter about rural towns and cities. He comments, disapprovingly, that some people "have, it seems, fallen for the 'big is good' mindset of the world and as such, unconsciously contributed to the 'rural is less important than urban' mindset" (Brain 2009: 105).

This book focuses on rural decline in Australia, with particular reference to Tasmania. We provide an analysis of the cultural context through an examination of secularization and pluralism, post-modernism, and cultural framing. A combination of these social and cultural factors shape the lives of the four rural Anglican communities of faith described in this study.

The study draws on theorists such as Weber, Berger, Drane, Lyon, Bouma, Ammerman, and Finke and Stark whose work tends to arise from, or cross the boundaries between, sociology and theology. Although this study is sociological, given the subject matter investigated, it is not possible to demarcate the theological (that is, the cultural aspects of the faith groups) from the sociological. The study is richer for working somewhat across disciplines. The four main dimensions of our theoretical approach to the study are: rural decline, secularization and pluralism, postmodernism, and cultural framing.

1. Rural Decline

In many ways the four rural communities of faith described in this book are typical of rural towns in Australia that have experienced significant structural changes over the past few decades. These social and cultural changes have had a significant impact on the Anglican Church. We focus on the period from 1996 to 2008 because this is the timeframe during which the events in this book took place.

The decline of rural communities is endemic in Australia. In *Smalltown*, a study of one of Australia's smaller rural communities, Ken Dempsey (1990: 301) observes that 'Smalltownites' have "become increasingly apprehensive about their future. They are sobered by the growth in unemployment, the decline in small-scale manufacturing industries in rural Australia, and their first-hand experience of such decline in this community." Similarly in *Making a Life,* Ani Wierenga (2001: 14) points to the same factors operating in a rural town in Tasmania: "the effects of changed economic conditions within labour and industry, structural unemployment, and the winding back of the public sector." She further notes that these processes are common in Australia, but "perhaps nowhere are the changes to social infrastructure more pronounced than in rural communities" (Wierenga 2001: 14).

The historical alignment of the Anglican Church with the middle and upper classes is becoming increasingly unsustainable (Cowdell 2004), and this is particularly so in Tasmania where rural decline and poverty are endemic. Tasmania has the lowest weekly household income in Australia, 17% below the national average; fully 34% of rural/remote Tasmanians currently live in low income households, which are in the bottom 20% of the national distribution of people ranked by their gross household income (Australian Bureau of Statistics 2003). Vinson's report (2007) into the distribution of disadvantage in Australia highlights the high level of economic disadvantage in many rural Tasmanian regions due to unemployment, low income, and prison admissions.

In the decade leading up to the parishes adopting ESM, between 1991 and 2001, the Diocese of Tasmania experienced the second highest fall in weekly attendance amongst any diocese in Australia, with a fall of 33%. The average fall in weekly attendance over the same period for the Anglican Church across the whole of Australia was 7% (Brighton 2004). This indicates a fall in those who actually attend the Anglican Church, rather than those who are 'nominal', in so far as they describe themselves as Anglican for the purposes of the Bureau of Statistics' Census, but do not attend church. In addition, the Diocese of Tasmania also had the second highest rate of nominalism at 32.4%, whereas the average percentage of nominal Anglicans in 2001 in rural dioceses in Australia was 19.5% and in urban dioceses was 19.8% (Brighton 2004). Of the 160,000 Tasmanians identified as Anglican in the 2006 Census, Harrower (2009: 204) notes that "Sadly, only 3,000 of them would find themselves in Anglican worship centres on any Sunday morning." The National Church Life Surveys (2001, 2006) indicate a decline of 15.6% in church attendance by Tasmanian Anglicans between 2001 and 2006. In 2001, a total of 2786 attendees in the Anglican Diocese of Tasmania completed survey forms for the National Church Life Survey, whereas in 2006 a total number of 2350 attendees completed survey forms. The changes are further exacerbated by the ageing of Anglicans. In 2001, 77% of all Anglican Tasmanian attendees were aged over 50 (NCLS 2001). The equivalent percentage for the Australian population is 32%. This age skew can be found in virtually all mainstream denominations. This is an issue that is very difficult for a diocese such as Tasmania.

The repertoire of options typically applied in the rural context to parishes in Tasmania that are deemed to be financially marginal is traditionally as limited as they are predictable. They usually include, in the first instance, the closure of individual centres, where towns no longer exist or have virtually vanished as has often happened throughout rural Tasmania. After closing centres, the next option is often to amalgamate the parish with a neighbouring one – and then to do this again as often as is required to create a viable stipend for the stipendiary priest. These two options have tended to be unsuccessful and subsequently, in this situation, the stipendiary priest is required to go from a full-time position to a part-time position. If this, too, proves to be unsuccessful, as has often been the case in Tasmania, then supply clergy (who are usually retired or honorary clergy serving in another parish) are enlisted to provide services on an *ad hoc* basis (such as providing Sunday services and pastoral care when needed). This option, too, has often proved unsuccessful as, by then, the life of the parish almost ceases to function. This pattern has been repeated again and again throughout Tasmania, as well as across Australia.

2. Secularization and Pluralism

Throughout the 1960's and 1970's many theorists conjectured that secularization was chiefly responsible for the changing nature of modern society (Berger 1967). Such theories, very broadly, are concerned with explaining why organized (Christian) religion is steadily declining in modern societies. Berger initially saw pluralism as being a side effect, or "twin phenomenon", of secularization (Berger 1969: 17). However, Berger (1992) now sees pluralism (and pluralisation – that is, how pluralism impacts on people's lived experience) as being the most significant effect of modernity upon society.

Bouma (2006: 5) claims that "it is essential to correct a misapprehension that dominated the late twentieth-century discussion of religion and secularity: secular societies are not irreligious, antireligious or lacking in spirituality". In Australia, this manifests through the emergence of a multi-faith and diverse society (Bouma 2006). This has resulted in a society where "religion and spirituality have seeped out of the monopolistic control of formal organisations like churches" (Bouma 2006: 5).

Modern Western society is pluralistic, where rival definitions of reality compete with each other for a share of the 'market' (Berger 1967). This pluralistic situation requires that different definitions of reality not only compete but also 'co-exist' with one another (Wuthnow *et al.* 1984). Pluralism in the West can be said to have issued in an era in which, on the whole, the church is no longer the predominant shaper of a belief system where values, morality, and community and personal identity are defined by adherence to, or attendance at, the church.

Contemporary society, because it is characterized by pluralism, provides more than one world-view to its citizens, and often these world-views are in competition with one another (Berger 1969). Pratt (2005: 192) considers the ubiquitous nature of pluralism in contemporary society impacts on religion in a way that demands acknowledgement:

> Plurality names the context of our so-called postmodern life. It names the contemporary situation of religion in society: religious plurality is a fact of our time. Plurality cannot be avoided. Neither can it be factually acknowledged then cognitively shunned, except by enacting a most obtuse denial. The social fact of religious plurality impinges today in a new sort of way, demanding a cognitive response: and it is this sense that it may be perceived afresh as a particular element of our time and our global weltanschauung.

Pratt's comments emphasize the fact of plurality in the contemporary world and the necessity of open response. For churches to fail to acknowledge pluralism is for them to deny the reality of contemporary Western society. At both a local and national level, such acknowledgement should inform decisions and practices of churches. The transition from churches holding a hegemonic position in society to one characterized by individual choice has major implications for the way that individuals determine their world-views and meanings:

The traditional parish system was predicated on a stable society where the church was at the centre of that society or, at least, played a significant part in the life of that society. The degree to which this premise has proved to be no longer applicable can be seen in the ethnographic descriptions of the four rural Anglican communities of faith that form the basis of this book. These parishes are no longer at the centre of the communities in which they are set. They are, in reality, on the edges of society. Yet, they have sought to re-invent themselves by seeking the well-being of those with whom they share their lives in the wider community and, in so doing, they have found renewed life for themselves, too. This process of seeking the well-being of the 'other' is a rather more respectful engagement with people than is the approach where the church assumes, as it did in the past and is still often the case today, that it is the sole bearer of truth. Pluralism does not have to be a cultural phenomenon that is antithetical to parish life. *Pluralism, if engaged with creatively, can bring new life and vitality to any community of faith.*

3. Postmodernism

In *The McDonaldization of the Church: Spirituality, Creativity, and the Future of the Church*, Drane (2001) argues that the evangelical wing of the Christian church remains closely aligned with the outlook of 'modernism' and that it needs to take into account the insights of 'post-modernism'. Drane's (2001) thesis is that the evangelical wing of the Christian church is a modernist movement that is essentially concerned with biblical literacy and has emerged as the church's response to the liberal humanism of the nineteenth century. In its attempt to keep up with highly educated, rational liberalism in the West, particularly in Britain and the United States of America, the church embraced an educated form of fundamentalism and sought to infiltrate the American graduate school system. This fundamentalism eventually evolved into its more palatable cousin, evangelicalism (Carnley 2004). The modernist emphasis on efficiency, calculability, predictability and control (Ritzer 1996) has been adopted by the church, hence the McDonaldization of the church. This has resulted in the control of faith in an understanding of church that equates faith with 'right belief', particularly of certain theological or creedal precepts that are taken and understood to be 'fundamental' (Carnley 2004, Drane 2001). Drane (2001) argues that by pursuing modernist principles and refusing to take account of post-modernity the church will be increasingly irrelevant to many in contemporary Western society.

Alternatively, Finke and Stark's (2000) analysis of 'winners and losers' in the American religious 'economy' argues that the degree to which mainline churches are sidelined depends on how much they have "rejected traditional doctrines and ceased to make serious demands on their followers" (Finke and Stark 2000: 1). Finke and Stark (2000) advocate a rather nostalgic view focussed on the past. Their solution is to regain certainty by adhering to modernist principles that have been interpreted as supporting 'traditional' Christian beliefs. They see post-modernity as the problem: the solution being a rejection of post-modernity and a return to the assumed certainty of modernity.

Finke and Stark's (2000) definition of 'winners and losers' is based on 'market' terminology. In defining 'winners and losers' solely in terms of the 'market', Finke and Stark (2000) succumb to the all too prevalent attitude (particularly in America, but being witnessed elsewhere) that 'success' equals 'big' in terms of the numbers of those attending church and the amount of money they give to the church. Such an uncritical acceptance of the 'market' as being the sole criterion as to whether religious institutions have 'succeeded' is premised solely on financial and numerical factors where success equals 'big' and failure equals 'small'.

Finke and Stark's (2000) analysis also uncritically accepts the close relationship in America between religion and politics, especially between conservative religion and conservative politics. It is a relationship based on power – it is based on who is perceived to be successful and who is strong and who shows leadership to rectify what are viewed as the 'wrongs of the world'. This reflects Finke and Stark's (2000) uncritical acceptance of the 'market' as being the sole criterion as to whether religious institutions have 'succeeded' or not. Finke and Stark's analysis does not adequately consider factors to do with social and cultural context, such as plurality, secularization, post-modernity, and demographic changes.

A 'success' oriented agenda is 'marketed' throughout Australian churches through conferences extolling the 'purpose driven church'. That is, the 'purpose' (programme) is to increase numbers who attend church and the amount of money they give to the church. Interestingly, in this model of church expansion, no account is taken of giving to other people/organizations/groups. The issues of poverty and/or rural decline affecting the church (Lyon 2002) are also absent in such an agenda. 'God's will' is presented as being the desire to make everyone financially rich. Monetary wealth equates to 'spiritual' riches in this type of 'purpose driven church' (Bearup 2003, Lohrey 2005, Lyon 2002, Simons 2007).

In Drane's (2001) opinion the church has become irrelevant to the post-modern world because of its alignment with modernism, which is why the numbers of those attending churches has fallen in most Western countries.

The lack of influence of the church is not related to people not wanting a spiritual component in their lives but is directly related to many churches failing to engage with post-modernity. For example, the Anglican Diocese of Tasmania is predominantly evangelical in outlook (that is, theologically conservative), even to the extent that it has become a 'Missionary Diocese' and there is widespread acceptance of the 'purpose driven church' agenda. However, there is still almost universal decline in attendance in its parishes and a lack of wider influence within society.

In contrast, Drane (2001) argues that it is important to creatively engage with some basic assumptions about the emerging post-modern paradigm:

1. there is a preference for learning by discussion and guided experience;
2. there is a desire for decisions to be made through group consensus rather than being based on instruction manuals or policy guidelines;
3. there is a rejection of simple, universal solutions;
4. there is a distrust for hierarchy, authority, and dogma;
5. there is an interest in accumulating experiences rather than formal knowledge;
6. there is a new openness to non-scientific ways of knowing truth; and
7. there is a new tolerance of different points of view – except those held dogmatically.

Perhaps Drane's (2001) most poignant comments relate to those who are most disadvantaged by the McDonaldization of the church – the desperate poor. Drane (2001) argues cogently for a spirituality that can engage with human vulnerability, without exploiting or manipulating those who are vulnerable. Both Drane's (2001) and Placher's (1994) emphasis on vulnerability echo Berger's (1992) optimism about the demonopolization of religious traditions within modern society.

There is another 'solution' to church decline. It is simply one of engagement: engagement by the church with social and cultural context, rather than resistance. This is both challenging and liberating. It is liberating in the sense that there is an acknowledgement of the influence of poverty and rural decline upon the wider society, which has likewise impacted upon the church. It is also liberating as it frees those who, through no fault of their own (that is, faithful parishioners and priests who feel guilty because they have 'failed' in growing their church numerically and financially), are caught in situations over which they have no control. It is challenging because it requires finding ways of being church that are life-giving (for the church and wider community) and which are contextually sustainable.

Post-modernity presents challenges to everyone, and it seems that the church is particularly challenged. Engagement, rather than resistance, in a creative and spiritually supportive way is the healthiest way for the church to respond to post-modernity. The form that such responses take may be many and varied, but this study demonstrates that the ESM model has proved sustainable, healthy, and grounded. The very malleable nature of ESM makes it highly suitable to adapting to the fluidity and change that characterize post-modernity in a way that brings enrichment to both parish and wider community and encourages in parishioners an outward focus rather than an inward focus.

4. Cultural Framing

Theology (that is, church culture) is critical in shaping the Anglican Church's response (that is, its action) to rural decline and to the post-modern social and cultural context in which it is located. The parishes described in this book have done remarkably well given their prior long-term decline. This is due to the outward focus that ESM has promoted in these parishes. By engaging with their context, as opposed to resisting it, the parishes have achieved a compatibility with, and support of, their wider communities that was not achievable under traditional stipendiary models of church. The latter become so focussed on raising money to pay the priest's stipend that the living out of their Christian faith is consequently curtailed and devoid of relationship. In making possible an 'elective affinity' between theology and context, ESM has facilitated a renewal of these parishes and the care shown by parishioners to those in the wider community. ESM, as an alternative way of being church, has encouraged a flowering of these parishes who have, to use the terms of those such as Ammerman (2001), Cray (2007), and Bouma (2006), contributed to the social and spiritual capital of their wider communities.

Weber argues that culture shapes the way that people act in response to particular social contexts. Weber (1976) developed this idea in *The Protestant Ethic and the Spirit of Capitalism* and, as Giddens (Weber 1976: 8) outlines in his introduction, Weber's study "is 'a contribution to the understanding of the manner in which ideas become effective forces in history', and is directed against economic determinism."

The underlying Weberian orientation of this book reveals that church culture, in this instance an inductive, sociologically informed theology, shapes social organization and action of the parishes. In the four case studies, the response of the parishes to a changing social and cultural context has been through ESM, which has enabled these parishes to engage with and respond positively to this context because of the conceptual framework undergirding ESM (that is, theology). How the church responds to its social and cultural context is a crucial factor in its viability and health. ESM is a model of church that has instituted and encouraged in these four communities of faith an 'elective affinity' between their faith position and the wider community.

The importance of response to context is perhaps the single most significant issue this research reveals. It is not the wide social and cultural changes that have taken place in the West, which have obviously had a marked impact on the church, that are crucial. Rather, the *response* to these changes is crucial to understanding the circumstances that many churches find themselves in today and their likely options. In other words, the focus needs to be on *response* to change not *change* itself. Social and cultural changes are important. However, it is the response to these changes that is most revealing and most critical in elucidating the place and role of the church in contemporary Western society. The stories of the four parishes in this book reveal the traditional model of church, based on a stipendiary priest, to be problematic in the current social and cultural climate, at least in these places. On the other hand, the parish stories reveal ESM to be enriching of parish and wider community in the current social and cultural context.

The four rural Anglican communities of faith described in this book now have a sustainable future in each of their particular contexts. Other models and ways of being of church have not been able to achieve this level of sustainability. The reason for this is a combination of both theological (that is, church culture) factors along with social factors. Ammerman (2001: 5) claims "the context alone explains a great deal" in that the social setting of a community of faith is more important than its theological orientation. However, we suggest, as we discuss in Chapter Six, that parishes with an inductive, sociologically informed theological orientation are more likely to engage with their context in a way that seeks the well-being of the wider community as opposed to being primarily concerned with internal issues such as raising the stipend for the stipendiary priest. This is borne out by the four case studies, which demonstrate the connectedness and care that the parishes exhibit towards their wider communities. These parishes have become, to use Ammerman's terminology (2001: 360), "congregations as connected communities". The quality of life and care within the community of faith of one person for the other is also enhanced and enriched where this theological orientation is manifest.

As such, the underlying Weberian orientation of this study is predicated on relationship – a relationship between faith community and wider community in which care of the latter by the former is paramount. There is an 'elective affinity' between post-modernity and ESM. What allows this affinity is that ESM is an incarnational church (a church that is grounded in the reality of its context) as opposed to a 'purpose driven church' (a church that is grounded in its own reality). Ammerman (2001) argues that, in a general sense, healthy congregations are able to be identified by their engagement with the wider community and by their capacity to incorporate new members into the community of faith.

Bouma (2006: 28) makes an appeal for an Australian pattern of being religious and spiritual which is grounded in an Australian context and relates to an Australian social setting:

> Nor is this Australian pattern of being religious and spiritual to be judged as inadequate by any other than Australian standards. The whingeing of Australian evangelicals about the level of biblical knowledge or church attendance among Australians is to judge an Australian institution by the standards of the American religious institution, as they were once judged according to British and Victorian standards. Why should Australian patterns of religiosity be judged by American standards?

The theological/religious challenge, then, is to re-vision and re-create the church in such a way so as to be an authentic manifestation of the church's true nature and role within society when, in service of others, it brings forth life, love and being (Spong 2001). A major issue with the evangelical model of church that is primarily based on a purpose-driven agenda is its complete failure to acknowledge the relevance of social and cultural context. Australia is not America, and nor is a small rural Tasmanian community (or a small Tasmanian urban community, for that matter) the same as Sydney or Melbourne in terms of demographic factors such as population, unemployment, aging of the population, and services. Megachurch models may well suit Sydney or Melbourne with populations of, respectively, 4.5 million and 4 million but Hobart has a population of some 207,000 and even the whole Tasmanian population is only about half a million. What may work well in one context may be completely unsuitable in another context. Churches *can* become "effective generators of 'social capital'" (Ammerman 2001: 362) but only if they engage with their social and cultural contexts rather than resist such contexts.

In the Tasmanian Anglican Diocese, there is a prominence accorded to the 'purpose driven church' model and a number of conferences have been held to promote this emphasis in ministry on increasing numbers and financial giving. However, to transplant from a different context (such as Sydney) into the Tasmanian context is a venture that is doomed to failure. This then results in parishioners and clergy feeling they have failed, when in fact the failure has been in failing to acknowledge context. For example, two Anglican parishes in Tasmania have run a '40 Days of Purpose' programme that *claims* the average growth in attendance at worship will be 20% and that the average increase in group attendance will be 102% (*Purpose Driven* website 2006). The *actual* outcome of running this programme produced results of 0% growth in both attendance at worship and group attendance!

Related to this issue is the matter of exclusivity versus inclusivity. This also arises from engagement or non-engagement with social and cultural context. Church models based on a conception that they hold the Truth, an exclusivist position, will have difficulty embracing other expressions of spirituality, whether these be other churches, religions, or New Age spiritual groups. As Bouma (2006: 28) comments, for "church leaders to complain that religion is being supplanted by spirituality is but for them to complain of the loss of their market shares in the religious economy". The expression of the faith position of such exclusivist churches is one of proselytizing: that is, mission as conversion rather than mission as service and care. ESM, as practised in the four parishes, displays a strong sense of mission as inclusive service of others and care of all those in need.

Conclusion

A sophisticated understanding of social and cultural context is central to understanding the experience of contemporary churches. The stories of the four rural Anglican communities of faith described in this book are contextualised within the reality of the lived experience of the communities in which they are situated. Sensitivity to social and cultural context also explains why ESM has worked as a way of being church in contrast to the failure of a more traditional way of being church based on a stipendiary parish priest, despite the context being the same.

Compared to other Tasmanian churches, Tasmanian Anglican churches consist of more older people and more women, and have smaller congregations. However, they are more likely to be involved with the wider community and, interestingly, still have a moderate level of newcomers (NCLS 2001, 2006). Given that the Tasmanian population tends to be older and poorer than other Australians it is not surprising that the Anglican Church in Tasmania reflects these demographic trends (Australian Bureau of Statistics 2002).

In comparison to their neighbouring parishes that share similar demographic and socio-economic contexts, the four rural Anglican communities of faith described here have experienced the longest period of sustained stability, growth, and health in their most recent history. This flourishing is demonstrated by such factors as the following: giving outside of the parish to support school chaplains, stable leadership, and the capacity to engage with and to care for the wider community. This has occurred because adopting Enabler Supported Ministry as a way of being church is a homologous response of these parishes to their context. Following Bouma's (2006: 168) discussions of "the interconnectedness of theology and sociology", we argue that ESM is a way of being church that is both sociologically and theologically apt.

Chapter One: A Theology of Enabler Supported Ministry

Introduction

The theological conceptual framework outlined in this chapter provides an interpretative framework for Enabler Supported Ministry (ESM) and enabling. The study draws on both the disciplines of sociology and theology. The theological context augments the sociological context addressed in the previous chapter. First we define Enabler Supported Ministry through five aspects that encapsulate the basic theological elements characterizing ESM. Second, we define the type of theology that characterizes enabling through a discussion of three understandings of ordained ministry. This provides a brief introduction to the theological framing of ESM and enabling.

A Theology of Enabler Supported Ministry

All forms of mission and ministry are shaped and formed by theological conceptual frameworks. ESM is not an 'odd' phenomenon, somehow outside the normality of Anglicanism, and nor are other forms of mission and ministry inferior to ESM. Five main areas together constitute a theological framework of ESM: mutuality, service, relationship, praxis, and Baptism.

1. A Trinitarian theology of mutuality

The Athanasian Creed asserts that, with reference to the members of the Trinity, there is "neither confounding [of] the Persons: nor dividing [of] the Substance" (Anglican Church of Australia Trust Corporation 1995: 836). This allows for mutuality and mutual deference between the members of the Trinity because they are three distinct beings ("neither confounding the Persons") all bound together in unity ("nor dividing the Substance").

There is no sense of subordination in the Trinity as they are all different, but one (Carnley 2004, Giles 2002). The relationship of mutuality that exists between the members of the Trinity might best be defined as 'friendship' (Pickard 2009). This applies to the life of the Holy Trinity and also to our life together. All are invited to share in this relationship of sociability and friendship between God and one another as God in Christ proclaims, "I have called you friends" (John 15:15). ESM draws strongly on this theology of mutuality in its valuing of all people and in its emphasis on sharing and friendship.

2. A Christology of service

A theology of service is based on the model of Jesus

> who, though he was in the form of God,
> did not regard equality with God as something to be exploited,
> but emptied himself,
> taking the form of a slave,
> being born in human likeness.
> And being found in human form,
> he humbled himself
> and became obedient to the point of death –
> even death on a cross.
> (Philippians 2: 6-8.)

This theology of service (based on an incarnational Christology) shapes the attitudes and practices of those who call themselves Christian so that, rather than being primarily concerned with orthodoxy, there is a sense of unity based on orthopraxis – a unity which recognizes diversity and which affirms the individual gifts and talents of each person.

This attitude is one of expansiveness. Given that God is a relational Being, our relationships one with another may be deemed 'godly' in so far as our relationships bring about life, love, and being. What we do matters. Pickard (2009: 236) relates service and mutuality to expressions of collaborative ministry:

> Perhaps friendship and servanthood are companion categories for ministry and leadership. As such they are given in and with each other. They are not simply different options that present themselves for appropriation. Nor are they simply complementary forms of ministry. Rather they inhere in each other; they too are 'one of another'. Together friendship and servanthood make collaborative ministry what it is and inform the manner in which it is undertaken. This means collaborative ministry is forever a fragile and suffering ministry that lives by trust and joy. It is the way in which Christian disciples learn how much indeed they are 'one of another' faithfully following the pioneer ministry of Jesus Christ.

In ESM this emphasis on servanthood and friendship can be discerned in the way that ESM parishes seek the well-being of others, whether within the church or outside the church. In addition, this ministry tends to be fragile in that it is not based on power or privilege. However, this fragility is also its strength: a strength that comes from following Christ's way of love and service.

3. An Ecclesiology of the Body

In ESM, as in the Holy Trinity, can be seen a capacity to hold together unity in diversity and diversity in unity. This understanding of the relational nature of the Trinity is used by the church to understand how the various members of the church have an underlying unity despite their diversity. The early church used the metaphor of the 'body' as a means of understanding how "they were the body of Christ and individually members of it" (1 Corinthians 12: 27) and that "the body does not consist of one member but of many" (1 Corinthians 12:14).

Indeed, this self-understanding in the early church was universalized so that all people are seen to be united as there "is no longer Jew or Greek, there is no longer slave or free, there is no longer male and female" (Galatians 3:28). This radical understanding of the unity of all people is reflected in the ecclesiology of the 'body' and is expressed in ESM through care of all people. In ESM, gifts, in all their varieties, are affirmed and nurtured and all these gifts are given for the common good. This common good includes both members of the community of faith and members of the wider community.

4. Action/Reflection (Praxis)

Within ESM, the fostering of a process of reflecting on action has been a central conceptual characteristic that has been useful for thinking about training and education. The process of reflecting on action is referred to as 'praxis', thinking and action (Freire 1973). It can also be described as the 'hermeneutic spiral', doing and then better understanding (Heidegger 1962). In the ESM model of being church the on-going training of Team members and parishioners utilizes praxis in that reflection on action is a central component of this education and training.

With reference to the dialectic relationship in training and education between understanding and policy/action (based as it is on the concept of 'praxis') the focus is on the process and not the product. Rice and Ezzy (1999) refer to Cornwall's argument that actively engaging in a process of learning helps local people to realize what they know, and that their knowledge is valuable; this in turn empowers them to be able to more effectively take control of their situations. Therefore, praxis is the reflective moment between theory and lived experience (Ackrill 1973). As a method of gaining insight, praxis is crucial to a growing sense of relating theology to practice and to a growing understanding that the process is more important than the product.

5. Baptism

The Christian community has, over the past few decades, reclaimed the primacy of the sacrament of Baptism as being the foundation upon which Christian identity and mission are shaped (Dowling 1997, Macquarrie 1972, Sofield & Juliano 2000, Sinden 1978). This understanding of Baptism has been crucial in the development of ESM because it affirms that all people are equal and are joined in Baptism and that who they are and what they do has worth.

An understanding of the significance of Baptism for Paul and the early Christian community begins with the account of Jesus' Baptism given in the Gospels:

> Jesus ... was baptized by John in the Jordan. And just as he was coming up out of the water, he saw the heavens torn apart and the Spirit descending like a dove on him. And a voice came from heaven, "You are my Son, the Beloved; with you I am well pleased". (Mark 1: 9-11)

In Galatians 3: 26 to 4: 7, Paul speaks for the first time of "baptism" (3: 27). At the time of their conversion the Galatians received the same Spirit poured out upon them by the risen Christ. It was this Spirit who created a bond of consecration between the Christian and Christ, and so between the Christian and all those already in communion with Christ. To each Christian, God says: "You are my beloved child; with you I am well pleased". Baptism is a sacramental initiation into the family, who can say to God, along with Jesus, "Abba! Father!" (Galatians 4: 6b).

As part of the theology underpinning ESM, Baptism is both a reminder and a challenge to live a life following Christ. In addition, the sacrament of Baptism is a source of education and training that constantly speaks of valuing the worth of the other.

These five defining aspects of ESM provide both a theological understanding of ESM as well as an understanding of how it can be lived out by members of a community of Christian faith. Being a member of the Christian community demanded, and still demands, that all relationships come under the scrutiny of the gospel. Relationships have to be lived in a new way, permeated by love. Nowhere in Paul's letters do we find a direct critique of the injustices that existed in the slave system or between the sexes. What is found, however, is a powerful concentration of attention on Jesus, the way he lived and the way he died, and especially the love that he revealed on the cross. Such a perspective could not but profoundly affect the behaviour of the early Christians. Likewise, this orthopraxis is pivotal in ESM as members of the parishes seek to live lives consistent with the life of Jesus.

The Anglican Church has committed itself to being a church in which the mission of God is expressed in word and deed (*The Anglican Communion Official Website* 2005). This requires a commitment to live in such a way so as to bear witness to the great love of God for all people expressed through the life and ministry of Jesus Christ. ESM encourages Anglicans, as Christians, to both become and live the Kingdom of God. This results in a life that bears witness to the radical, liberating, and redeeming work of God. Members of the church are affirmed and equipped "for the work of ministry, for building up the body of Christ, until all of us come to the unity of the faith and of the knowledge of the Son of God, to maturity, to the measure of the full stature of Christ" (Ephesians 4: 12-13).

As Christians seek to become and live as Kingdom of God people there is always the risk that their words and deeds may diminish the degree to which the Kingdom of God is manifest in their midst. Such oppressive practices as slavery, although sanctioned by both state and church, eventually came to be seen as inconsistent with the values of the Kingdom of God. Likewise, the church is seeking to be entirely transparent with regard to its structures and practices which have led to the abuse of people (be it sexual, emotional, verbal, physical, or spiritual) within its care. Such abusive behaviour is entirely inconsistent with the values of the Kingdom of God. Furthermore, it may be necessary for the church to take a prophetic stand against damaging culturally defined roles. For instance, in Australia the treatment of Indigenous people and asylum seekers continues to test the relationship between the state and the church.

In the future, the church needs to avoid practices and structures that diminish the degree to which the Kingdom of God is manifest. If it does not then it effectively diminishes the degree to which it is able to be a bearer of the good news of God's love for all people as expressed most fully in the life and works of Jesus Christ. Within ESM, there has been an intentional emphasis on a process that affirms and supports and respects. In a sense, it is a creative mission of healing and seeking wholeness. This theological basis is described in another context in the words of Fichandler (2002: 33):

> *Tikkun Olan.* In Hebrew, "To repair the world". We are the only animal who strives to do that. It's our creative mission. And this mission gives us our identity.

The theology that forms the foundations of ESM is centred on its mission of inclusivity and care of all people. It is a mission of creativity and healing, and is expressed through:

1. relationships – that they might be permeated by love;
2. structures and policies – that they be just and equitable;
3. liturgy/worship/prayers/music – that they be life giving and inclusive;
4. language and attitudes – that they be affirming and nurturing;
5. (on-going) theological and pastoral education – that people both become and live the Kingdom of God. To achieve this there needs to be:
   a) reflection on the context in which God has set people; and
   b) discernment and nurturing of the gifts which God has given each person;
6. engagement with society – that it be truly and inclusively engaging; and
7. concern for creation – that the beauty of the earth and all creation be truly valued and conserved/preserved.

A Theology of Enabling

Enabling requires an expanded conceptualization of what constitutes ordained ministry. Enabling is essentially defined by a theology of collegiality. This section addresses two understandings of ordained ministry: ontological (thesis) and functional (antithesis). By way of seeking to resolve the impasse that exists between these two different understandings, we offer a synthesis of these understandings of ordained ministry, which involves an understanding of the emerging role of enabling.

1. The Ontological Understanding of Ordination (Thesis)

The Biblical verse from Psalm 110 (4b), "You are a priest forever according to the order of Melchizedek" was, and perhaps still is, the Biblical reference *par excellence* to describe the ontological nature of ordination. That is, in the rite of ordination, one's being is changed (referred to as the 'indelibility of Holy Orders'). Or, at least, one's will is considered to be graced by God. After the exhortation and examination of the ordination candidate the bishop prays:

> May God who has given you the will to do these things give you the grace and power to perform them. Amen. (Anglican Church of Australia Trust Corporation 1995: 795)

Another way of understanding the ontological nature of ordination is that ordination is iconic. In the debates regarding the ordination of women to the priesthood in the Anglican Church of Australia, it was argued by some that because Jesus was a male then only males could be priests. This is a very similar argument used by those who support 'headship'; namely, that as head of a church/parish/diocese the ordained person needs to represent the ideal type that those who hold this view support. If the ideal is of a male God, then priests need to be male. Likewise, if the understanding of headship is that of power and authority then the head will need to be powerful and authoritative.

Rather than an emphasis on power and authority, spirituality can remain vulnerable, as God is vulnerable (Placher 1994). A vulnerable God, as is seen in the life of Jesus, is one who shares the human condition, including suffering and death. An understanding of God as being vulnerable offers another perspective to the ontological type of argument that sees God as being all-powerful. Any perspective on life is socially constructed (Berger & Luckmann 1966), as is evident in these two understandings of God (God as powerful and God as vulnerable). Either perspective of God arises from different viewpoints that are determined by social and cultural context. Some find the pluralistic situation where there is only provisional truth, as opposed to absolute Truth, to be a frighteningly unsettling proposition. It certainly upsets the notion that the true meaning and understanding of priesthood can be determined. Nor is it possible to determine what the True source of what the priesthood, as an icon, is meant to represent. This focus on an ontological understanding has probably more to do with Platonic thought than with the God revealed in Jesus.

The priesthood is deserving of respect (Carnley 2001, 2004) and it is not our intention to diminish or fail to appreciate, respect, or honour the ministerial priesthood. On a personal level, Rev Collins loves being a priest and thanks God for being called and given grace to live out this ministry. However, following Küng (1980a, 1980b, 1983, 2001), his concern is with the type of argument used to justify the ministerial priesthood (or to diminish lay ministry) based on the notion that there is one True source of our understanding about the nature of ministry in general and ordained ministry in particular, both within the early church and the contemporary church.

Küng (1980b, 1983) considers that there was 'pluriformity' (as opposed to uniformity) in the early church with regard to how it was structured, with how ministry was undertaken, and by whom. Dunnill (2001: 25) states that the early church had a "*threefold pattern of ministry*", being the "universal, local and congregational". Because 'pluriformity' was a distinguishing mark of the early church it should therefore remain a mark of the contemporary church, too (Küng 1980b, 1983). This is because any form of church that focuses on 'office' rather than on 'ministry' is mis-representing the standard which Jesus sets as an example to follow; a standard that is based on "*diakonia*, 'service' (really 'waiting at table')" (Küng 1983: 486). Therefore, there was not ever, nor is there now, one True way of understanding ministry in general or ordained ministry in particular.

2. The Functional Understanding of Ordination (Antithesis)

We will now address the second of the two understandings of ordained ministry that were referred to earlier. Many years ago, James Collins remembers listening to a programme on Radio National (ABC Radio) involving an interview with the Religious Studies scholar, Joseph Campbell. In the interview, Campbell described Christian clergy as being 'functionaries of the church'. Campbell went on to suggest that clergy can be viewed this way because they simply perform various functions prescribed by the church.

One tradition within the Anglican Church claims that the functions of an ordained person, priests in particular, are to absolve, bless, and consecrate. There is nothing wrong with these functions; indeed, there is a great deal that is good in them. Another tradition sees the priest as being the minister of 'word and sacrament' (*Verbum/Sacramentum*). Some might restrict this to being a minister of the word alone. Others suggest that the priest is the 'gatherer of community'. Again, this is entirely laudable. Given these various functions attributed to the role of the priest, can such functions be used to define priestly ministry? Other people do preach, gather community and, within some traditions, celebrate Holy Communion/the Lord's Supper/Eucharist. Though one might question the validity of these functions if presided over by someone who is not ordained the question remains, however, are priests defined solely by what they do (Sherlock 1997)?

Those exploring their calling to ordained ministry and those seeking new appointments as ordained ministers are considered against certain criteria. Generally, what happens when selection committees meet to consider the attributes (that is, functions) they look for in a new candidate/appointment is that they develop a list of functions or a job description. This might appear to be a very sensible thing to do at one level, but at another level it has never been clear just what these functions should be and it is always very ambiguous, depending on who draws up the list. This is the situation that Cowdell rightly describes as "managerialism: leadership minus faith and imagination" (Cowdell 2004: 211).

Sinden (1978: 293) makes the point that the "essence of ordination" has changed considerably over time. Likewise, Sherlock (1997: 149) addresses the difficulties of defining ordained ministry, particularly in the contemporary context:

> The context of much ordained ministry has changed from that of supporting Christians in a largely 'Christendom' environment to enabling them to survive, function and reach out in and to a world that knows little of the gospel of Christ. The churches in Australia are called more to missionary than maintenance mode, and the ways in which ordained ministries are exercised in this context is growing in variety.

Therefore, as with the ontological understanding of ordained ministry, based on there being one True way of understanding ordained ministry, the functional understanding of ordained ministry also encounters serious definitional problems. This results from the pluriform ways in which ordained ministry is expressed and, as Sherlock (1997: 149) rightly reminds us, "the ways in which ordained ministries are exercised in this context is growing in variety".

So, then, what do we look for in leadership within the church, both lay and ordained? We suggest a synthesis of these two understandings of ordained ministry that involves an understanding of the emerging role of enabling would be a reasonable way of proceeding.

3. An Understanding of Ordination as Enabling (Synthesis)

The discussion of the two understandings of ordained ministry outlined above has explored the tension between the 'catholic' view of the ontological status of priesthood and the 'protestant' view of the functional status of priesthood (or 'ministers'). Most people face a tension between being and doing. Enabling can be understood as a manifestation of being a priest that breaks through this tension and reconciles both the why (being) and how (doing) of being a priest/minister.

We are not suggesting that enabling is now the one True way to express an understanding of ministry in general and ordained ministry in particular in the contemporary Western world. Rather, as we look at the type of leadership that we might expect within the church, the conceptual framework of enabling allows for pluriform expressions of ministry in general and ordained ministry in particular.

Carnley (2004), Küng (1983) and Cowdell (2004), amongst many others, each speak of the *charism* necessary for leadership within the church. For Küng (1983) the primary focus is one of service and collegiality. As with Sofield and Juliano (2000), we consider that gifting, sharing power, enabling, mutuality, and respect for the 'other' are at the heart of being a priest. Being an enabler is about allowing God's people to be who they might be as, in the words of *A Prayer Book for Australia* (Anglican Church of Australia Trust Corporation 1995: 780), they "'take their part'... in partnership with other clergy and the congregation". This applies as much in a parish, as in a school, or as at home; anywhere, in fact, where people are called to live and move and have their being. Being a priest, whether in the traditional sense or as an enabler, involves expressing the *charism* of service to others in all areas of life.

The Anglican Church is uniquely positioned to cope with pluriformity. The Anglican capacity to embrace catholic and protestant, word and sacrament, and to hold together unity in diversity and diversity in unity means that Anglicans can readily engage with the pluralistic situation in which they find themselves in contemporary Western society. The capacity of the Anglican Church to engage with pluriformity also allows it to value both ordained and lay ministries. Macquarrie (1977) highlights this collegial approach to ministry:

> In the liturgical renewals of recent years, care has been taken to ensure that the laity have a definite active role in the worship of the Church along with the clergy – this is *concelebration* in the broad sense. In the reforms of Church government likewise, a larger voice has been given to the laity – this is the principle of *collegiality*, again in a broad sense. But if these reforms are to be meaningful, the laity must also have a voice in the development of the Church's doctrine – there must be *co-theologizing*, if I may coin a word. (Macquarrie 1972: 18, see also Macquarrie 1977: 420 ff)

Such an emphasis on collegiality and the valuing and celebration of both ordained and lay ministries is central to ESM. Indeed, ESM, as an alternative way of being church, specifically fosters an egalitarian view of all ministries, in which no one ministry is viewed as better or superior to another, but merely different.

In addition, ESM is a contemporary example of pluriformity in action, and can adapt to various contexts. ESM can be seen as a synthesis between the ontological understandings of ordination as focused on 'being' (ministerial essence) and the functional understandings of ordination as focused on 'doing' (ministerial roles). Further, the practice of ESM engenders an environment where parishioners, and particularly the Team members, participate in a process that allows for the on-going development of, and reflection on, contextualized theologies (that is, a type of 'co-theologizing' in practice). In its inclusive and expansive ethos, ESM allows the institutional church to be relevant to the pluralistic, secular, post-modern world without losing the traditions of Anglicanism and the central concepts of Christianity.

Conclusion

This chapter provides a theological conceptual framework for understanding Enabler Supported Ministry and enabling. It identifies five defining theological characteristics of ESM (mutuality, service, relationship, praxis, and Baptism) and the theological emphasis in enabling on collegiality. The adoption of an inter-disciplinary approach provides an understanding of ESM and enabling that combines both sociological analysis as well as theological insight. Such a framing offers the possibility of appreciating the inductive, sociologically informed theology that underpins ESM and enabling. The stories of the four parishes in Chapters Two to Six demonstrate that new forms of church that are aware of both social and cultural context and theological context facilitate healthy and sustainable communities of faith that are connected to their wider communities.

Chapter Two: The Parish of New Norfolk

Introduction

The Parish of New Norfolk became the 'guinea pig' for exploring and implementing the development of Enabler Supported Ministry (or Collaborative or Mutual Ministry or Total Ministry as it was variously known) because of two main factors. One is its proximity to Hobart that allowed for frequent and quick trips by the Enabler (to begin with, the Diocesan Ministry Officer), who was located in Hobart. During this 'teething stage', reasonable commuting time was a considerable advantage to both the Parish and Diocese as the feasibility of ESM was examined in depth. The Parish of New Norfolk also happened to be the first parish to commit to explore and consider ESM as a possible option of church ministry. Hence, it was in this Parish where the process of ESM was initially worked out and modified as this 'working-out process' progressed. Although ESM was somewhat simultaneously explored in other parishes, it was in New Norfolk that a great deal of time was spent sorting out the details and possibilities for what finally became known as ESM.

The implementation of ESM as a new way of being church with the help of the Diocesan Ministry Officer took almost six years to come to fruition. This chapter outlines the process of exploring and developing ESM at New Norfolk. This process then became the 'working template' for the way ESM was implemented throughout the Diocese, although it was modified in response to new ideas arising from reviewing the procedures developed at New Norfolk and to the individual needs of other parishes exploring ESM. This chapter focuses on the process for implementing ESM and serves as an introduction to ESM by way of highlighting the homologous response of ESM parishes to their context.

Background

New Norfolk is a unique rural community nestling in the Derwent valley. The town is situated on both sides of the River Derwent, a major river in Tasmania, and the source of most of Hobart's water. It has retained its own character, despite being only a comfortable half an hour drive from the State's capital, Hobart. In any other Australian State, New Norfolk would be considered an outer suburb. It is a spectacularly beautiful rural town, offering a combination of forests, farmland, historic buildings, waterways, and stunning scenery. The community of New Norfolk was historically dominated by skilled labour at the local paper mill, along with low-level white-collar work at the State's then psychiatric hospital. Most of these positions no longer exist and this had a devastating effect on the local community and upon the community of faith at New Norfolk.

The Anglican Parish of New Norfolk – A Description

The Anglican church of St Matthew's, New Norfolk, is the oldest church building in Tasmania. It was built in 1823 and Consecrated in 1825, though earlier buildings were incorporated into this structure. In hindsight, there seems to be a certain 'rightness', then, that this Parish was the first to embrace the process of exploring Enabler Supported Ministry as a new model of church ministry. This culminated in 1999, after a lengthy three-year period of consultation and discussion, with the calling of the first Team.

Since 1996, the Parish of New Norfolk had been unable to sustain a full-time stipendiary priest and the Parish was forced to sell the rectory to remain financially viable. Leading up to this time the town of New Norfolk and the surrounding district had experienced the scaling-down and eventual closure of the Royal Derwent Hospital (in 2000/2001), which had resulted in the loss of around one thousand jobs from what was, then, the State's major psychiatric hospital. There was also the need for fewer employees at the paper mill, due to increased efficiencies being implemented during previous decades. Before these reductions in the size of the workforce began, there were about one thousand five hundred employees at the mill. This resulted in the loss of over one thousand jobs at this paper mill alone. In addition, other positions were also lost from a nearby mill town, Maydena. As Ralph comments below, this loss of employment is indicative of the significant change that had occurred in just one small rural region in Tasmania:

> They would have had somewhere between one to two thousand people. It's been phasing out over the last 15 to 20 years [referring to the Royal Derwent Hospital].... They've gone from about 1500 employees down to about 400 now [referring to the paper mill]. Yes, especially with a lot of people ... retiring and as they retired they moved off to Hobart which meant some ... who were regular Parish attendees here, left and then started connecting up with parishes in town [that is, in Hobart]. (Ralph, business proprietor)

Because of this economic downturn experienced over a number of decades the town and district were considered by many to be an undesirable place to live. This reputation was only strengthened by virtue of the town having been the location of the State's major psychiatric hospital up until its closure in 2000/2001. People living in 'Norfolk' were considered by many as being mentally 'sub-standard' and easily put in their place as can be seen from the following comments:

> The Derwent Valley is under a cloud in some ways because of the past of the hospital, the Royal Derwent Hospital, that mental institution. And I had known through my sporting life, and through my connections within the justice section in the State, that New Norfolk people … can be put down and they struggle against that. And for people to come in and think, "I've got it right and I can tell you what." … I've seen that in everything. In the Police Force; I've seen it in the sporting teams and I felt it now and again in church too. You've got to be careful of that. They are special people. They're very welcoming people. You know, they've looked after me tremendously. (George, retired)

George's comment reveals not only the 'stigma' often attached by outsiders to people from New Norfolk, but that, despite this stigmatization, they were still a very welcoming people, particularly the New Norfolk parishioners.

The Parish of New Norfolk had been struggling for quite some years to maintain the stipend for their rector and, finally, in April 1996, the last Rector resigned and left.

> Well, I was told by people who had been at the church a long time that it was the quickest move they'd ever known. He was gone within a month. All I know, being Treasurer, there was, you know, we were strapped for cash. (George, retired)

This was a terrible conclusion to a long and difficult period for the Parish of New Norfolk. Having tried so hard to keep raising the necessary money to fund a stipendiary priest, it seemed like all their efforts amounted to nothing but failure.

> The people … were also pretty worn out by the constant demand to raise money, which had just about burnt them out. They loved their communities and their churches and wanted them to flourish but all their efforts seemed to be of no avail. (Claude, priest)

The latter comments aptly describe the worn out and depressed state of any parish coping with issues of sustainability and lack of money. Not only are such feelings and issues characteristic of parishes across Tasmania but also across Australia generally and many other parts of the world as well. They will inevitably arise where any parish is facing the harsh reality of financial non-viability and the prospect of possible closure coupled with a deep love for their church and community.

Options for the Future

Following the pain of having lost their rector and their concerns about their financial state, the Parish of New Norfolk then experienced a sense of collective shock from being told by the Diocese that they would not have another stipendiary priest appointed to the Parish due to the financial inability of the Parish to afford the stipend. After the initial shock, there were some important questions that needed to be explored by parishioners as to what, exactly, the future of the Parish might look like.

Until the appointment of a priest by the Diocese as the Diocesan Ministry Officer (DMO) in February 1998 the parishioners of New Norfolk, as George and Ralph explain, were largely left to their own devices and were struggling with mixed feelings of hope, loss, disappointment, regrets, and apprehension about the future of the Parish:

> I mean he [the last rector] left about April in '96. Mavis will tell that we didn't have communion for nine months. (George, retired) We were left out in the wilderness, really. Mavis and myself were both registered Lay Readers with the licence to be able to preach as well, so we could do Morning Prayer services but I think it was six months before anyone came to do a Eucharist. (Ralph, business proprietor)

This situation changed markedly with the appointment of the DMO. His role was to encourage, resource, and assist parishes to implement change. The DMO was able to work through the various options with the parishioners, carefully exploring each choice before a decision was finally made.

> I said I had come at the Bishop's request to explore options for the future. The options available were either closure or join with other churches in the wider community and forge an ecumenical partnership or continue to rely on supply clergy or consider the possibility of a new approach to ministry called local collaborative ministry which later was replaced by the term Enabler Supported Ministry. People seemed to be weary of the supply clergy solution – the clergy who came were often retirees or people no longer able to

> hold down a fulltime post. It was hit or miss as to whether a parish ended up with someone who would stay long or who had the skills to help make a difference and so increasingly this option became unattractive. (Claude, priest)

Several options for the future of the Parish of New Norfolk were explored by parishioners and the DMO. The first option was amalgamation with the neighbouring parish. This has been a favourite option of the Anglican Church employed not only in this Diocese but also around Australian and the Western world. It is also an option implemented by many other Christian Churches to solve the problem of declining numbers and finances. The neighbouring parish to New Norfolk is the Parish of Hamilton, which had already been amalgamated several times with other parishes over a long period of time to assume its current form. It was considered impracticable to expect the Hamilton parish priest to extend any further because of the vast size of Hamilton Parish, which covers the largest geographical area of any parish in Tasmania.

The second option was to join the parishes of New Norfolk, Hamilton, and Brighton together as a regional 'hub' in which these parishes would share two priests. This option was, in effect, no different to the first option as it simply spread two stipendiary priests over a vast area. Nor did this option (or the previous one) really address the causes of why so many parishes in Tasmania were experiencing similar issues.

The third option was for the Parish to rely on retired supply clergy. Such clergy would travel to the Parish to ensure that pastoral and sacramental needs were being met while the Parish was trying to decide which option was the best for the long-term future of the Parish. As George explains this is, in fact, what did take place for a while:

> [The supply priest] looked after Sunday services.... He looked after funerals, did some pastoral visiting and he was absolutely wonderful to us. Absolutely... and knowing his workload I just felt, "This isn't right". I mean, we all were sad when the parting came about but I just felt, hey, you know, we've got to love him and his wife too. And I don't think we were doing that by just asking him to come up.... I mean for a lot of people it was an easy way out. He was an ordained priest, you know, and all we were paying was his travelling money and I just didn't see this ... doing the right thing. So I know the saying

> goodbye to him hurt a lot of people. I don't like to see him go, though I mean we've kept the friendship going. But I felt it was the way to go. (George, retired)

It is testimony to some of the New Norfolk parishioners that, even given their dire circumstances, they could still respond to those trying to help them out with care and a grasp of the reality of the situation. It is these characteristics, particularly the willingness to address the social and cultural context of their Parish, that enabled the Parish as a whole to move towards a consideration of ESM.

The fourth option was for the Parish of New Norfolk to explore the possibility of becoming an Enabler Supported Ministry parish. This option would allow, given the parishes' financial constraints, for the sustainability of pastoral and sacramental life within the Parish. For some in the Parish this seemed to be an overwhelming responsibility to assume, whereas for many others this seemed to be a challenge that the Parish could realistically undertake. Some in the Parish also hoped that this would be an interim measure until the Parish could afford another stipendiary priest. Other people, as can be seen in the following comments, could not see how it was all going to work out:

> I remember Claude talking about it in church. I felt, at the time, that it was a band-aid. That it wouldn't make us a real church, so to speak, because we wouldn't have that leadership, sort of. And talking to him [Claude] and he said, "What do you think about it?" I said, "Oh, I don't like it at all. You know, I can't imagine how it can work properly. I can't imagine having 'pretend' priests and I can't see how it will work". Therefore, I was very negative. There are other people in that Team that could see the vision and could see it very clearly and knew that that was the way that we could be sustained and how we could grow. But I just couldn't see it. (Sonya, retired)

Sonya's comments are representative of the common reaction of some parishioners to ESM. They simply could not see how it could work. Moreover, they looked on ESM as providing 'pretend' priests, or 'microwave priests', who are not really priests. There is a sense, stemming from centuries of parish churches having assumed a certain model of stipendiary ministry based on a priest, that there is only one 'proper' way of being church. However, the financial crisis that spurred New Norfolk to consider options other than the traditional stipendiary model was a 'blessing in disguise', even though it was scary and different, as the DMO reflects:

> In the first instance, church finance was the driving force. It's probably true to say that ESM is less likely to have happened had there either been a re-distribution system of resources in the Diocese or had the parishes themselves had the capacity to sustain their own life. I don't think they would have naturally chosen this because of the dominance of the existing paradigm that served the church well for centuries. No one finds change easy. The sheer pain of change and going through the transition processes are not welcome by most people. So, the financial crisis really did play out powerfully in causing people to think the unthinkable in terms of how they might go about things. That's what drove parishes out of what had been a place of comfort and rest to a new place. I would also call the process a work of God's Spirit among the people. (Claude, priest)

This is a strength of ESM. It acknowledges that change can be frightening and is often resisted and challenges those seeking a way forward to consider what to many appears to be 'the unthinkable'.

ESM: Process, Issues, and Context

New Norfolk was one of more than half a dozen parishes that chose to consider ESM. The Diocesan Ministry Officer's appointment in February 1998 brought significant change to the Diocese of Tasmania as the hope of moving forward began to become a concrete reality for many struggling parishes, particularly in rural areas. As a new model of being church, the process of how to engage with parishes in an exploration and discussion about ESM was developed very much 'in process' and always in relation to the issues and contexts of the parishes concerned. This reflects the homologous response of ESM to social context as well as cultural context.

The DMO "sought the help of others from the wider Anglican Communion who had adopted the paradigm [ESM types models] and had some years of experience and many lessons to share with us" (Claude, priest). Drawing on such advice, a step-by-step process was shaped that developed as conversations with parishes interested in ESM unfolded. The first part of this process was called the 'Enquiry Stage', and it was followed by 'Seed Sowing' and 'Calling Out' stages. These are discussed below, with specific reference to New Norfolk, detailing the experience gained from the early days of developing this process with a number of parishes across Tasmania. This would establish the process subsequently used by the Diocese when parishes chose to explore ESM.

1. 'Enquiry Stage'

This first stage encompassed all discussions and activities associated with the consideration of ESM by a parish, and were consultative and exploratory in nature. The insights of the then DMO are worth quoting at length because the process that unfolded at New Norfolk became the model for the implementation of ESM throughout the Diocese. The geographical proximity of New Norfolk to Hobart meant that this process was very much fine-tuned at New Norfolk and given depth to a degree simply not possible with some other rural parishes that were many hundreds of kilometres from Hobart. In describing his initial approach to parishes, the DMO emphasizes respect and a sense of travelling 'with' these parishes and not 'against' them:

> This approach is not about manipulating anybody. It's not about imposing anything upon anyone because that's a violation of the creation, of personhood, and the communities themselves which had already experienced manipulation, suffering, and pain. I deliberately sought to come alongside and to be a companion in the process of exploring what might be possible in their circumstances, taking very seriously the nature of each context – the uniqueness, the differences, the diversity. It seemed to me to be important for the story of each community to be heard and my task in part was to listen and help facilitate the telling of the story. I simply kept on going back to the six communities that had been identified as being most likely and willing to want to talk and explore a different way forward. Well, no, it was more than six initially, but it came down to six eventually. (Claude, priest)

That so many parishes in Tasmania were considering ESM is a reflection of the serious problems facing the Diocese in 1998. The situation has worsened since then. However, the consultative nature of ESM allowed these parishes to look at ESM as an option, but not to feel pressured to adopt it. The decision to adopt ESM or not always resides with the parish, not the Diocese. That is, ESM is a 'ground-up' way of being church and not an impositional model. It is an essential characteristic of ESM that it not be imposed from 'above' but that it develops, under diocesan guidance, from 'below'. The DMO specifically clarifies that some parishes chose not to pursue ESM, and this was an option supported by the Diocese if that was the considered decision of a parish:

> It's probably worth making the point that there were one or two parishes that actually journeyed for a while but concluded, "At this point in time, we can't see that Enabler Supported Ministry is the way forward for us", and we said that was fine. I felt it was important that people didn't feel they'd let someone down by saying no to ESM, and that the time of enquiry was a good experience. So we tried to bring the conversation to an end in a way that allowed them to move on and do what they felt was the right thing to do. (Claude, priest)

The Diocesan Ministry Officer also makes the observation that these changes affecting the church are, however, a part of a more general decline in rural areas:

> Some of these communities had lost almost everything. Important community services were disappearing: local schools, hospitals, banks, and businesses were closing down and relocated elsewhere. It almost seemed the last straw to lose the church as well. Somehow or other the church had managed to be there, through the many twists and turns, and were trying hard to find a way of avoiding closure. (Claude, priest)

In such circumstances, it can be difficult to suggest something new. Indeed, amidst such decline, feelings of sadness and fear about the future, nostalgia for the past, coupled with resistance to change, frustration, despair, and exhaustion make it as difficult for the person suggesting something new as for those people to whom the suggestion is made (even when they chose to consider new and alternative options).

Given such complex emotional factors as well as the reality of rural decline and financial limitations it is imperative that the process of exploring ESM as an option for the future be slowly and carefully undertaken. This was a crucial role undertaken by the DMO, as Claude explains:

> The Enabler Supported Ministry option … was presented to parishes as a possibility requiring careful explanation because no one really knew anything much about it. So I offered to spend some time with each parish exploring and explaining the theological basis and practice of ESM and what it would mean in their situation if they

> adopted it, so that they could make an informed decision whether to adopt it or not.... We called the work we did with the parishes the Enquiry stage. We said that we would take as much time as each church community needed to reach a mind about ESM.
>
> My role as Ministry Officer was to hold that process as much as possible against any attempts to hurry it along. I knew there was a sense of urgency but at the same time we wanted everyone to participate. No one should be left saying at the end of the process, "it was never explained to me" or "I was never asked my opinion". (Claude, priest)

One of the most important aspects of this 'Enquiry Stage' was allowing the process of storytelling to unfold in each parish considering ESM as a means for acknowledging the past, accepting the realities of the present situation, and reaching out to the future. Central to the facilitation of this unfolding process of 'story' was the role of the DMO and, later, the Enabler:

> The task of the Ministry Officer and Enabler in the enquiry process is to be alongside, creating space for enquiry, and allowing people to tell their story. I am convinced that in some cases, without the telling of the story, it would have been very difficult if not impossible for the parish to move on at all. The telling of the story can be a releasing moment because people can celebrate what had happened and put it behind them. It moves a parish towards the making of a decision and, in the end six parishes chose the enabler ministry option.
>
> The process requires deep loving and caring. All of this work is strongly relational. That is what life and faith is all about. It's about being able to say – "whatever you decide is okay, we respect your choice, we will continue to support you whatever you choose", no coercion. One of the things that Enablers often tell you is how important it is for them to be a non-anxious presence in the communities they serve. They're not there with any agenda other than that of being a good companion, facilitator, and affirmer. (Claude, priest)

Allowing the parishes looking at ESM time to tell their stories and own them allowed parishioners to not only be able to move forward but to also deal with often a lot of pain and hurt, even anger. The DMO also makes the point that sometimes there was resistance. This was worked through openly and honestly, with respect and awareness of underlying anxiety, or even anger:

> At times, I did meet some hostility as well as hurt in churches I worked with. I heard some pretty sad and desperate stories about things that had happened to them; the poor way in which decisions had been made and how some things had been imposed upon them. Some had not been allowed to make their own decisions; instead, decisions had come 'from above' in the form of 'father knows best'. This is so contrary to the whole notion of shared ministry, and a distance away from wholesomeness.
>
> So it was a matter of learning to work in contexts with fairly high levels of anxiety, where people often needed to express their anger and other feelings of hurt. It was also important to have moments of celebration, special occasions marking the contributions that others had made in preparing congregations for this journey and process. (Claude, priest)

In some parishes, such as New Norfolk and St Helens, the last Rector, realizing the implications of their poor financial states, made significant contributions towards the parishes becoming more self-reliant:

> Within the limits of the traditional paradigm that they felt obliged to work with, they had nevertheless been able to encourage people to do things consistent with the enabler ministry paradigm. For example, in some places the gifts of the laity had already been identified, developed and were being exercised among the people to good effect. They had already created a sense of community, hospitality and belonging, working and ministering together. (Claude, priest)

Nevertheless, ESM was so very different to the traditional model of church that strong resistance was perhaps inevitable. Indeed, sometimes there was such a level of resistance that in addressing it the option of changing tack and even closing had to be 'named' as a real possibility. The radical nature of ESM was difficult for many to cope with and in all parishes considering ESM there were periods of resistance, as Claude describes:

> At times, it was backs to the wall. We said, "we're going to have to address this opposition, or we'll go down". But they had been given a choice, and it was okay to decide to do other things, even

> close. We kept saying, "you can have a good ending, a tremendous celebration. It's okay to say no. You can move on into something else". (Claude, priest)

ESM emphasizes collegiality, not authoritarianism. Enablers to ESM parishes are not heroes, who come in to save the day. Rather, they facilitate a democratic 'grass-roots' approach to being church. As the DMO outlines below, the ethos of how ESM is not about wielding political power but is about being vulnerable can resonate with those who have lost power:

> My experience in the many different situations of marginalisation and poverty was that of God's power being known and experienced in weakness. And so, in situations of powerlessness and great vulnerability, with fairly high levels of suspicion and anxiety and yet a deep desire to do something and be faithful to God (situations where people for so many years had maintained a faithful Christian presence and witness in their communities), we set out to see whether God would move to bring something new and different and more wholesome and life-giving.
>
> So that's what the journey was about and that's the ethos we tried to maintain in the communities as we journeyed together, aware of the anxieties of others in the wider diocesan system. (Claude, priest)

The nature of ESM permitted not only recognition of the need to respect difference but also to embrace context. In this way, the reality of local conditions to do with demographics of rural decline and the theological foundations of Christian ministry fused into affirmation of individual worth and connectedness with each other and those in the wider community. In his work with parishes looking at ESM, the DMO saw and encouraged this process of building a community of God that is also very much a part of the wider community:

> It's about recognizing that all the gifts are present already in the context for the church to be the church. It's not about importing something into a context but the releasing of something already there. It's about laying the foundations of a community of love and respect, openness and trust, risk taking and affirmation – a community that believes God is present and at work in each person and that there's a whole well of love and life to be drawn from every individual. It's about a release of latent energy within the life of the

> gathered church and into the church as it reaches out in love and concern to the wider community.
>
> So that is the frame of reference for ESM. It's about being the body of Christ together and in the world. It's about no person being alone in ministry. It's about leading together, worshipping together, holding the 'word and sacraments' … together. It's about embodying the life of God in Christ in ways that are appropriate for each community in their context. (Claude, priest)

In New Norfolk, parishioners discovered in ESM not only a new way of being church that incorporated them all into a relational model of faith, but also a powerfully empowering and democratic model of church ministry. ESM, because it is a 'ground-up' model, acknowledged the reality of their financial state, the decline in the community of New Norfolk, their worth and gifts as members of God's church, and their place as a parish in their township and surrounding districts. The lengthy process of enquiry had facilitated a thorough exploration of ESM and a careful discernment process. From a parish characterized by despair, hopelessness, financial constraints, disappointment, and exhaustion the 'Enquiry Stage' into ESM revealed the possibility of a new future for themselves. It was a daunting future and a risk – ESM is, after all a very different model, and New Norfolk was the first parish to actually choose it. There was no other parish in Tasmania to use as a guide and mentor. This must have been a scary decision.

2. 'Seed Sowing'

In August 1998, the New Norfolk Parish Council decided to ask the Diocese to allow the Parish to develop the Diocesan vision for local ministry within the Parish. Having made this decision, the Parish of New Norfolk then became the 'ESM trial parish' for the stage-by-stage implementation of Enabler Supported Ministry as a new way of being church.

Within the Parish of New Norfolk, the commitment of the Parish to implement the development of ESM was marked by a 'Seed Sowing' service in October 1998. In this important service, every member of the Parish planted seeds as a symbolic way of making a commitment to this new way forward. This service also involved parishioners making a public reaffirmation of their Baptismal Vows and a commitment to develop every member ministry within the Parish. The intention of this service was to recognize the giftedness of every person in the Parish and to recognize that each person had a vital role to play in the life of the Parish and the wider community.

The emphasis in ESM on all members of the church developing their gifts in a corporate living out of their faith was, in many ways, quite a re-direction from traditional Anglican Church models. "It is very much a shift away from a culture of father or mother knows best to a community of radical equality" (Claude, priest). Some parishioners found this exciting as Ralph describes:

> It was exciting because somebody was actually taking notice of what we'd been asking for so long, to come and try and find a way that we can still be church within the community. Not in the old way but in a new way, and it was exciting. Being able to work within the community, with the community and as a group together. Not having a single person within the parish trying to run the parish, but a group of people together, working as a team, that have got different areas and different gifts that we're able to use in different ways. (Ralph, business proprietor)

These changes were not always easy as members of the Parish now had to take on more responsibilities and to make decisions formerly left to the parish priest. Most people in the Parish accepted this new way while a few still hoped that the old ways would eventually return. The process unfolding at New Norfolk was similar to the way the process was unfolding elsewhere throughout the Diocese. Although the process of implementing ESM in the Parish of New Norfolk was a learning experience for all concerned, some found it easier to accommodate than others did. But as it evolved, ESM also developed its own momentum:

> Once the new paradigm had been explained and embraced – once people got beyond the decision making stage and were into the stage of formation and beginning to live it – then many things fell into place and pattern of life began to emerge.
>
> For some it was natural because they were already doing it, but collectively, as a community, as a body it was very new because they had never really been given the permission to be the church in entirety – they were always in a state of dependency upon ministerial supply through imported clergy. And indeed, there weren't the kind of structures within the Anglican Diocese of Tasmania to allow for

> that development up until that point in time. It was new territory. (Claude, priest)

It is noteworthy that this emphasis in ESM on all members of the church living out the Christian message according to their gifts was something that some parishioners found resonated with how things worked in the world outside the church. This is one example of how ESM facilitates an 'elective affinity' between theology and social context. Such people were building on their experiences of how things operated elsewhere, as Claude observed:

> Some people were drawing upon experiences and practices in their places of work or organizations that were steeped in collaborative ways of doing things. These people felt that the church was actually catching up with the normal way of life and leadership in these organizations, which were already communities of equality and mutuality, where people are given space and responsibility to make decisions and to work collaboratively in teams. (Claude, priest)

3. 'Calling Out'

In August 1999, a year after the 'Seed Sowing' service, the Parish had a 'Calling Out' service during which the Parish nominated five members of the Parish to become the Local Ministry Support Team. The role of a Local Ministry Support Team (LMST) is not to do everything needing to be done within the Parish but to be trained in all aspects of becoming the incumbent of the Parish (albeit a shared incumbency and not a solo incumbency). As with the other parishes examined in the case studies, those 'called out' not only represented the community of faith but they also reflected the demographic make-up of the wider community. At New Norfolk this manifested itself in that those 'called out' to serve on the Team were mostly locals with just a few people who had not been born in the town or district. The composition of the Team has changed over the years and now there is an even balance of people who are locals (that is, born and bred in the town or district) and those who have moved into the town or district more recently (as New Norfolk became an attractive satellite town for Hobart).

The role of the LMST is to train and nurture others to be able to use their gifts for the good of the parish and the wider community. This double focus of seeking the well-being of both the parish (the community of faith) and the wider community defines something of the ethos of Enabler Supported Ministry as can be seen from the following comments from two parishioners:

> Well, now, where do I start? Okay. (Laughs gently.) My contacts are with the choir. I sing in a local community choir so that's a contact for me and I've been involved in the community house with little things there, so that's a contact. I'm also on the ACCESS committee. Which looks at roads and footpaths for people who are disabled. Access to things; buildings, toilets, public toilets, shops, all that sort of thing. I don't know. I seem to be everywhere. I hear in the street, people call out, "Hi, Lola. Hello Lola." It's very beautiful. (Lola, retired)

> I guess you're a leader but also you're a representative. So you are like a shepherd but I don't think I'm as wise to be a shepherd. I am still a representative of the people and part of the ministry in a Team like this is having everyone part of that ministry.... I would like to see it as a big circle with us in the middle reaching out around to the others. (Sonya, retired)

The Local Ministry Support Team at New Norfolk needed to develop expertise in people skills, conflict management, and leadership styles and also to expand their theological training. There was a second Calling Out in August 2000 that was intended to affirm the members of the Local Ministry Support Team and to decide which members of the Local Ministry Support Team would co-ordinate the various roles required for the running of the Parish. These roles included ordained ministry, administration, funerals, prayer, pastoral care, and baptism. Team members took their work seriously and learnt about their roles as they assumed these responsibilities, as Sonya describes:

> I think that our responsibilities were shown to us as we went along. Things that we thought we could never do, we did. I can remember standing up and preaching for the first time with so much concern and worry. I don't ever underestimate that we've got a huge responsibility. You can't preach to people and preach something that's not quite right. You can't do a funeral if you haven't got a heart for the people. There's nothing that you can do in church on a Sunday if you haven't – if you're not convinced that it's right. (Sonya, retired)

Over these years, the Parish of New Norfolk began to increasingly take responsibility for every aspect of parish life and parishioners were trained by the Enabler to lead worship services, too. This involved intensive preparation for assuming the responsibility required of these roles; namely, preaching and leading worship, along with intercessions, reading, music selection, and helping with Holy Communion. George comments on the multi-faceted role of leadership that the Team shares and the recognition of the burden placed on stipendiary priests:

> Well, having been five of us there and seeing what needs to be done I just think, "How on earth can one person do this?" I know wives move in and do some of the other church work but I would have felt the stress for one person. Although they're trained. You know, like they're going to be able to put sermons together far quicker than what I ever could. That was one of my stresses in the ministry but I really did fall into Team Ministry very easily. (George, retired)

As the members of the New Norfolk LMST began the long process of learning how to be the incumbent, they found themselves doing things they would not have thought possible years earlier, as Sonya explains:

> So we've learnt a lot. You know, to think that we'd ever do funerals. To think that we would ever do a lot of the things that were so important to other people. It just seemed out of the question before and now we're doing them and God has been so gracious to us because he's taught us. You know, the Holy Spirit's been with us every step of the way. Times when you get frustrated. I guess you get frustrated in life. I mean it's just part of it. But I believe, as a Team, we are very responsible to the people but we're also responsible to each other because we can appreciate where each other's talents are. None of us have got the same talents I don't think. We might overlap but we're all very different people and I think we can appreciate where the others are coming from. (Sonya, retired)

They also embraced the living out of their faith in relationships with other parishioners and with those from the wider community. This was a relationship characterized by equality and community, as Lola describes:

> No. No, it has nothing to do with bossing. The words that spring to mind are "By the people, for the people" and I'm not sure whether that's a communistic expression, so forgive me, but it really does say what it is. It's ministering to the people by the people and it's not just confined to a church. It happens as we walk down the street, as we shop. Today, of course, I've done a funeral, been involved in a funeral. Many people there, I've been involved in funerals for their family

> and we meet again at the church. These friendships come all the time and every time you meet them, in the supermarket, the butcher's or whatever, there's a conversation happening and that's what it's all about. (Lola, retired)

The connectedness that ESM encourages in Team members, and parishioners generally, facilitates a markedly different way of being church compared to the traditional model of stipendiary priest. A stipendiary priest obviously does have a valued presence in the wider community of the church in which he/she serves. However, in parishes where this is no longer possible, the ESM model not only enables this presence and connectedness in ways simply not possible from other options such as a supply priest but also in ways that are reflective of a "radical equality" (Claude, priest).

The responsibility that the Local Ministry Support Team undertakes in being Commissioned for their role is a significant responsibility. As Ralph comments, the Team members are careful, with the help of the Enabler, to ensure that they each get adequate time off to spend with family and friends and that they are not being burnt-out by virtue of being a member of the Team:

> Well, I've been in full-time employment as well, so time was limited what I had available to be able to spend in the church working, but it meant that if I was unable to do something there was someone else that was able to do it. That's been a wonderful thing with a Team because if I haven't been available, somebody else has been available and if they haven't been available I may have been available or somebody else. So we're not reliant on one person only.
>
> [B]ut any time that we feel that it does get too much for you, you can back [away] a bit for a while and say, "Look, I need to have a couple of weeks' break". You can have your couple of weeks' break to re-fuel yourself; the Team still runs, the Team still exists and the parish life still goes on. Then the person, when they're ready to come back on board, they are able to come back on board and feel refreshed and go ahead, rather than anybody being burnt out. We've got that ability. (Ralph, business proprietor)

Furthermore, the strength of this team approach is that when tragedy struck the Parish of New Norfolk in the sudden death of its only priest (Ordained

Team Member) it was able to cope with this terrible loss, keep going, and bring about a sense of recovery and health for the Parish and community.

In July 2001, the Diocesan Assessment Team and Safe Ministry with Children's Panel visited the parish. Every member of the Parish was allowed to express how they felt that the changes were going and, further to this, every member of the Local Ministry Support Team was interviewed individually by the Assessment Team and also by the Bishop. They were also screened for work with children. The latter is a requirement for ministry in any Anglican church in Tasmania, and Australia generally, and all potential Team members are screened in the same way as any priests are before appointments can be made. Because of child abuse cases in the past, the Diocese of Tasmania has a particularly rigorous screening process that also includes Australia-wide police checks. The outcome of this Diocesan and Episcopal visit was that the Parish of New Norfolk was endorsed to continue to develop as an Enabler Supported Ministry parish.

On 30 August 2001 two members of the Local Ministry Support Team were ordained as Deacons and on the 14th of February 2002 the Parish of New Norfolk was commissioned as an Enabler Supported Ministry parish. This commissioning service was the culmination of an almost six-year journey, beginning in April 1996 when the last Rector resigned and with the depressing realization they could not continue as a stipendiary parish. Such beginnings did not auger well for their future, but from little steps and little beginnings something quite wonderful had blossomed – far bigger and better than any of the parishioners or Team members could have ever imagined all those years ago.

4. Reflection

Rev James Collins was appointed as Enabler to the Parish of New Norfolk on the 1st of September, 2001 and was privileged to share their journey with them for many years. One important aspect of ESM that became clear to Rev Collins in the early years of his work as Enabler to a number of parishes is that ESM is not a miracle cure for struggling parishes that appear to have no future and nor are Enablers miracle workers. Rather, ESM is about enabling others to fulfil the multiple responsibilities of an incumbent priest. The role of being an Enabler is to train, support, and allow the LMST to determine what they consider is best for the parish as can be seen from the following comments from George:

> [T]he Enablers allowed us to work through the ministry as to what we saw as valuable for the church, the congregation we knew and that's what I see the Enabler to do. Just to enable us to, you know, to look wider. If we start to get narrow to just make us look wider. And the training too; that is needed. And it is just to enable people to work in their own parish. (George, retired)

Another central aspect of ESM is its underlying characteristic of 'working with' rather than 'working against'. As ESM unfolded in New Norfolk there was a realization that this was a good way of being church and, as so often happens in life, a sense of amazement that it hadn't been thought of earlier:

> But with time, some started to say ESM is a bit like working with rather than against nature, that it felt like they were working more with God than what they'd been doing before. It seemed a much more natural and wholesome way of being church because the previous paradigm tended to produce a culture of dependency and co-dependency.... So there is a wholesomeness in ESM, and as people were released into the paradigm it became part and parcel of the way of being and doing things, and people felt really good and said "Why didn't we see this before?" (Claude, priest)

As George suggests below, there is an overwhelming sense of optimism about the future of the Parish of New Norfolk. Having made the change to become an Enabler Supported Ministry parish out of economic necessity the Parish now considers this to have been the correct choice and would not seek to revert to any other form of parish organization or church model. George speaks for many parishioners from New Norfolk when he expresses not only what to many Anglicans, especially those in the church hierarchy, may well sound like revolutionary fervour but a recognition that parishioners may well have things to teach priests:

> To me it's been something else. I think it was very early in the piece ... that we said, "Well, what we're experiencing now, we wouldn't like to go back to one priest". We just got this feeling that we were being allowed to express ourselves more and, you know, you wanted to give out God's word to people. I think I once said it was like I'd love to shine the light of [the] Lord round at the High Street. And I think, (laughs), I think the stipendiary priests have got to *grow* in that thought too. (George, retired)

The combination of optimism, a sense that ESM is an excellent model of church, and a recognition that ESM enriches their community of faith has resulted in a parish that is quite certain it made the right choice in choosing ESM. And not only would they never want to revert to the former traditional model of parish ministry, they have grown so much in themselves as Christians that they stand confidently as the embodiment of this new way of being church. They feel it is a far more democratic and outward expression of their Christian faith than was permitted in the traditional model. The traditional model of the stipendiary priest ministering to the parish flock can produce a "culture of dependency" (Claude, priest), although in some contexts it may be the best choice. The parishioners of New Norfolk have found themselves empowered and privileged through ESM: they 'know where they stand' and that is in a new place of service and sharing and they carry out these roles faithfully and responsibly. ESM has fostered a deeper and stronger connection with the wider community than previously existed because ESM allows for an engagement with the cultural context of their faith and the social context of the demographics of rural areas and the pluralistic and secular world of post-modernism.

From having an inward-focus, being primarily concerned with fund-raising, the New Norfolk Parish now has an outward-focus on serving the wider community. This includes involvement with community groups beyond New Norfolk, such as helping with settlement programmes for newly arrived refugees and helping in a programme for a group of African women who are learning to sew and to cook (using ingredients available in Tasmania) which is held on most Fridays in Hobart. Every parish activity prior to the introduction of ESM was focused on fund-raising and the various groups within the Parish were even rostered to have regular fund-raising events. This was felt to be necessary as the financial burden faced by the parish required that almost every gathering of parishioners was a fund-raising event just so as to be able to meet the demands of raising money to pay for the full-time (or part-time) stipendiary priest. Sonya comments on this focus on fund-raising where parishioners

> used to have months for, like, Mother's Union to raise some money. We'd have the Guild do the fair. We had the Caritas have one month, so we'd have a dinner. (Sonya, retired)

This focus on money is crippling in its non-viability as a way of being church when the finances for a stipendiary priest are lacking. It is also nonviable in the sense of taking away energy, resources, and time that could be spent on Christian service and on actually living out their faith. It also saps creativity and outward engagement.

From having lost its sense of identity and feeling unclear about what role the community of faith might play in the wider community the parishioners of New Norfolk now have a strong sense of who they are as a parish and also of their place and involvement in all aspects of community life. For example, Sonya and Lola comment on how their church is completely integrated into the wider community:

> I see [the church] as an integral part of the community. It's not a 'them and us'. It's like it's an 'us'. Part of the 'us' doesn't always come to church to worship but that part of the 'us' is always reliant on the church, knows we're there, talks to us in the street. Every member has conversations with people and so it is, you know, still the body of the church in the community, but not every part of the body works the same way. (Lola, retired)
>
> This is the fifth year I've been asked to talk at the Dawn Service. People know that I'm representing the church. I don't want anyone to ever think that I'm there for me. Although, having said that, I'm proud that I'm the daughter of ex-service people. But you stand up in front of, once again, all these people, some that I went to school with, the Vietnam fellows I went to school with. I talk and say my own sentiments but then I pray and then I invite them to pray with me. To me, that's a huge extension of the church. This year there were more there.
>
> Ralph was at the 11 o'clock service. He prayed and read.... But we're there from the Anglican Church. We don't hide that. We are introduced as that.... But I think that's a privilege. Ralph said at church on Sunday, over the week we'd seen so many at a funeral, we'd seen so many at the services, and we're part of the church, so there's no brick wall. (Sonya, retired)

Furthermore, these quotes from Sonya and Lola suggest that the Parish is confident about the future and about being able to engage with the community as the community continues to change; for, indeed, the community is changing and continues to change. From having been deemed to be a town in which no one wanted to live, New Norfolk is now attracting a lot of people from the Australian mainland who see the beauty of the town (located as it is on the Derwent River) and its proximity to Hobart (an easy thirty minute drive) as being very desirable and are choosing to live there.

When Rev Collins began serving the Parish of New Norfolk as Enabler many shops along the main street, High Street, were boarded-up and those that weren't often had their windows broken and there was an air of gloom hanging over the town. New Norfolk is now seen as a very desirable place to live and High Street is now a very smart street and boasts one of the highest number of antique shops of any town in Tasmania (indicating the change in social status of those living in the town). As Sonya comments, changes in the town are bringing new people into the area from diverse backgrounds:

> I suspect that we're going to have a lot more people from interstate. People are moving over for various reasons; lifestyle changes, all sorts of things. I think that we'll see lots of people coming in, as we've started to see already. I think that we're going to be so easy to commute to Hobart from New Norfolk with the highway changes and all that. So I think that we'll have a lot of people coming from Hobart even, to live here. I think that this must increase our numbers, even if it's only a small increase. I think that we'll find that there will be people that are committed Christians that come to us. That can only enhance us and we can learn from these people. They're going to come from all different backgrounds. (Sonya, retired)

Adopting ESM has helped a struggling group of caring people find a sustainable and inclusive way of living out their faith in the context of the changed (and changing) face of the New Norfolk community.

Conclusion

The story of the Parish of New Norfolk 'gives voice' in a permanent way to their journey from despair and sadness and what looked like some sort of end to joy and celebration and new beginnings. It is a story of hope worth telling. It is also a story of courage because New Norfolk was very much the 'guinea pig' parish in terms of the exploration and introduction of ESM in the Diocese of Tasmania. Embracing change and difference in a new model of church ministry has breathed new life into this declining parish.

ESM, as a different and new way of being church, encourages all people to work together and nurtures their gifts, allowing them to participate fully in the life of their community of faith and in their wider community. Although the institutional church is marginal to many people in contemporary Western society, the community of faith at New Norfolk is now an integral part of the wider community and ESM allows this to happen. Sociologically we move from: a stipendiary priest model to ESM; the church being marginally relevant (or irrelevant) to the wider community to the church being more relevant to the wider community; tight budgets focussed on paying the stipend to giving and serving; hierarchical church to inclusive church ministry; an emphasis on power to an emphasis on relationships; and an inward focus to an outward focus.

In other words, the narrative of the community of faith at New Norfolk demonstrates how the theology of ESM shaped the response of the church, both local (that is, the Parish) and regional (that is, the Diocese), to rural decline and social and cultural change. This is consistent with an underlying Weberian orientation, outlined in Chapter One; namely, that theology (that is, culture) shapes action and that ESM enables an 'elective affinity' between theology and context.

ESM has been well received in both the Parish of New Norfolk and the township. It has led to a sustainable future for the Parish at New Norfolk, and the parish now makes significant contributions to the wider community, as far away as Hobart itself. This is because the theology and church structures of ESM fit with the structure of social relationships of the parishioners and the place of the church in the wider community; or, as Ruth maintains, this is because people are concerned about real existential concerns and issues:

> Real stuff. Stuff that's going to grab people. Reality – a *real* God that they can connect with and have a *real* relationship with…. You just live it. (Ruth, accountant)

A Chronology of Events

April, 1996: last full-time stipendiary Rector leaves Parish.

February, 1998: the Diocese appoints a priest (Claude) as the Diocesan Ministry Officer (1998-2002).

October 1998: 'Seed Sowing' service in where every member of the Parish planted seeds as a symbolic way of making a commitment to a new way forward.

August 1999: first Calling Out service to form the Local Ministry Support Team.

20th – 21st November 1999: Team members from the Parish of New Norfolk attend and spoke about Enabler Supported Ministry at the Parish weekend held at Camp Conningham by the Parish of Channel/Cygnet.

August 2000: second Calling Out service.

19th December 2000: Parish holds a vote to become an Enabler Supported Ministry Parish.

June 2001: Team members 'Called Out' to specific ministries.

July 2001: Diocesan visitation to Parish to determine whether the Parish was ready to be Commissioned (the visiting team included the Reverend Neil Vearing, the Reverend Sharon Green and Dr David Thomas).

August 2001: Ordination candidates interviewed by the Bishop.

30th August 2001: Ordination to the Diaconate of 10 people Called to Ordained ministry from five parishes (Channel/Cygnet, New Norfolk, St Helens, Circular Head, Sheffield).

1st September 2001: James Collins begins as Enabler to parishes of Channel/Cygnet, New Norfolk and St Helens.

3rd October 2001: James Collins Commissioned as Enabler to parishes of Channel/Cygnet, New Norfolk and St Helens.

14th February 2002: Full Commissioning of Parish of New Norfolk including the Commissioning of the Local Ministry Support Team (Celia Hooker, Ellen Sweet, Brian Eccles, Lyn Plunkett, Lance McCallum) and the Ordination to the Priesthood (Lyn Plunkett).

May 2002: The Diocesan Ministry Officer (Claude) leaves the Diocese.

9th July 2008: James Collins resigns as Enabler to the Parish of New Norfolk.

Chapter Three: The Parish of Channel/Cygnet

Introduction

This chapter describes how the introduction of Enabler Supported Ministry to the Parish of Channel/Cygnet led to renewed growth (from 7 or 8 people in worship on a Sunday to around 40 to 60 people in worship). Such extraordinary growth came about because ESM led to greater parishioner concern for each other and a greater engagement by parishioners with the community. This is a story particularly characterized by transformation. This chapter outlines how the 'Calling Out' process that was initiated at New Norfolk was modified at Channel/Cygnet to suit the local context. This modified 'Calling Out' process became the 'working template' for the way the process was subsequently implemented throughout the Diocese, although the nature of ESM always allows for adaptation to suit local context and need. Hence, it is probably true to say that ESM only ever has a 'working template' rather than a 'set template'.

The journey of the Channel/Cygnet Parish towards adopting ESM was much quicker than that experienced by the parishioners of the Parish of New Norfolk, largely because of what had been learnt about the early stages of the process as it unfolded in New Norfolk. In addition, New Norfolk Team members were able to act as pseudo-mentors to Channel/Cygnet, and they spent a weekend with the Parish of Channel/Cygnet explaining and talking about ESM. Channel/Cygnet, unlike New Norfolk, also had, for a short time, the presence of a rector in the Parish while ESM was initially being considered and explored, before he finally left due to lack of funds to pay him. Nevertheless, new things were learnt about ESM and modifications were made to ESM during the exploratory and formation stages in Channel/Cygnet. The malleable nature of ESM allows for this on-going fine-tuning and adjustment to suit specific contexts.

Background

The localities of Channel/Cygnet and the surrounding region have experienced considerable change over the past 50 years. The area surrounding Cygnet had been a traditional orchard area (hence the old 'nick-name' for the State of the 'apple isle'). But, as discussed below, this orchard industry collapsed and, at around the same time, beginning in the mid-1970's, the area began to attract 'hippy/alternative life-style' types of people. This trend has continued with 'tree-changers' now moving into the area. As a result, Cygnet is the location of the State's internationally renowned annual folk festival, the Cygnet Folk Festival.

Both the community generally, and the Parish in particular, have seen huge changes since the end of the Second World War. It used to be a fruit growing area, with the families who had settled there continuing to raise their families and to grow fruit. Bush fires in 1967 had a devastating impact, as did the downturn in the demand from the European Economic Community (EEC, which later became the EU) for Tasmanian grown apples. Then, more recently, there has been an influx of a diverse, cosmopolitan group of people choosing to live in the area.

Demographic changes led to a decline in the local population, then, subsequently, an influx of people moving into the district. But the newcomers had no link with the community or the parish. The Channel/ Cygnet region has experienced significant demographic change linked to significant cultural change. As a result, this combination of factors resulted in a situation where people were less inclined to join community groups (Putnam 2000) and where the phenomenon of 'believing' but not 'belonging' was evident (Davie 1994).

This process of change can be very tiring for people as can be seen in the following reflections by a parishioner:

> Oh, tremendous changes. The community, when I first remember it as a community, was very much a fruit growing community. Established families who had been in the area and had settled here in the early days and those families would continue to live in the area and work in the area and it was basically just that. A community of pioneers, who had established their properties here, had raised their families here and had continued to work in the area. But that, of course, changed quite dramatically probably about the '50s when we saw quite a change in the fruit industry where our traditional markets were lost. Also we had bad bush fires through in '67 which wiped out a lot of the properties. People lost very, very heavily and were forced to move away.
>
> So we went through those very dark patches and then the community took on a time where we saw people coming into the community to live as a suitable and desirable place to live. The community grew and

> sort of fitted in very well with some of the establishment that was still here. It wasn't completely wiped out but very, very heavily reduced and the people that came in seemed to fit in very well and we ended up with a very cosmopolitan type community and it's continued to grow and Cygnet, to me, has become a very desirable place to live, a lovely community to live in; a caring, sharing community. So, yes, quite tremendous changes; almost as diverse as we possibly could be, I think. (Sam, retired)

Sam, who is a long-term resident of the area and whose family were amongst the first to settle in the area, went on to comment that the traditional market for the local apples was the United Kingdom (UK). When the UK joined the EEC Tasmania was forced out of this market due to tariffs imposed by the EEC. The growers then had to re-plant to sell apples to the Middle East. During the 1950's and 1960's 70% to 80% of work in the area was with the apple growing industry coupled with some employment in the timber industry. Now all of these apple-growing farms have closed. For example, in Gardners Bay alone, where Sam lives, there were 22 farms and now there are none. Consequently, the employment associated with the apple industry evaporated (up to 500 to 600 people in the picking season).

The impact of this loss of population and employment had an extremely adverse impact on local businesses and services, with many closing or moving to other areas:

> I've noticed changes in terms of centralization. When we first moved here, what used to be the Cygnet Council had just been amalgamated into the Huon Valley Council and that manifested itself in withdrawal of services or less localised services. In the ten years that we've been in Cygnet, there were three banks when we first moved here. There's only one now. I think they all closed and then that one re-opened. (Sue, teacher)

As the farms began to close the shops began to close. These closures included the local chemist and the banks (three to none then, recently, back to one again). The local entertainment began to close, too, until the recent turn-around with people moving to Cygnet. Older families who had settled in the area began to leave during the 1960's through to the 1980's, and these families never came back. The impact of this level of decline on the local residents, and community in general, was profound and the remaining local residents could only watch in despair and hope for better days:

> Well, until we saw the change in the town where Cygnet became the type of town that people discovered was desirable to live in, we lost virtually all banking services. We had three banking services operating in the town at that time. It got down to virtually nothing. We lost our chemist shops; we didn't have a chemist shop. All entertainment type of thing went to the wall where we used to have theatre operating a couple of days, a couple of nights a week. That completely closed. There was virtually nothing to keep young people in the town at all, so we saw a huge exodus of young people that just had to move into the cities to try and find employment. In a lot of cases their families went with them because it seemed to be the only way that they could really keep the family together; to all move into the cities and try and find some suitable employment, some sort of suitable accommodation, which a lot of families did, and, unfortunately, we never saw those families back again. They just left. (Harold, retired)

The Anglican Parish of Channel/Cygnet – A Description

These changes experienced in the area had an obvious flow-on effect in the Parish. As with New Norfolk, the impact of rural decline, de-population, and lack of employment opportunities and services has a profound impact on the local community and the Parish alike. As Louise's comments below indicate, financial constraints within the Parish led to various amalgamations with other parishes and other administrative arrangements, none of which were successful:

> We were part of the Ranelagh Parish for a while. Ranelagh, Huonville and Dover; I think we were joined with them at one stage. Bruny Island was in with us at one stage and that didn't work. I can't remember all the details because I wasn't involved a lot with the church Parish Council *et cetera* then, but things would not go right or the different centres didn't get along, but it never seemed to work out. Then we came to having a part-time rector and even that was a struggle and it was going to be shut the doors until ESM.... but it was a blessing that we had it otherwise the doors would be shut. (Louise, retired)

As with the Parish of New Norfolk, the Parish of Channel/Cygnet was also unable to maintain a full-time stipendiary priest, nor a part-time priest for that matter. The cost of maintaining a stipendiary priest was an unsustainable financial burden on a numerically declining parish community. The implications of this situation were recognized by the Parish as is borne out by Sue's comments:

> Really, the catalyst for it was the fact that, and it was a fact and it was an agreed fact, that there was no future for the Parish in the traditional model. The priest who came after the amalgamation when the finances were such that we were even incapable of paying his stipend, he stepped back to a part-time appointment; he was a music teacher and he began teaching music in the local Catholic School. So he was working part-time and I think there was a recognition in the Parish that we couldn't really be or do what we wanted to be or do with that kind of an arrangement. (Sue, teacher)

The Parish of Channel/Cygnet has sought to engage with this change and, given that the change is continuing to occur, the community and the Parish will face on-going pressure to continue to 're-invent' themselves as circumstances change. On-going engagement with change is necessary for the continued health and viability of any church (Cowdell 2004). Thus, if the community of faith in Channel/Cygnet, and the community in which it is set, had any hope for a continued healthy existence they needed the resilience to participate in a process of engagement with change. Moreover, given that this is an area characterized by continual change this engagement with change is an on-going requirement for healthy existence.

Declining church attendance was an inevitable consequence of the drastic changes to the demographic makeup of the Channel/Cygnet area. The number of people attending church began to decline. This resulted, as it had done in New Norfolk, in considerable pressure to maintain a stipend. Amalgamations with other parishes consequently occurred, but none of these were successful. It was not until people began to move into Cygnet recently, coinciding with the introduction of ESM into the Parish, that the attendance at church began to increase again.

Over the same period that saw these large demographic changes there have also been cultural changes. The role of the church has significantly changed since the Second World War, hence even when the Channel/Cygnet area did begin to experience an increase in population it did not correlate to an immediate increase in church attendance. In the area in former times, church used to be more formal and there were three services each Sunday with a full-time priest servicing a number of centres (Gardners Bay, Lymington, Nicholls Rivulet, Cygnet and Garden Island Creek). Now only one centre remains at Cygnet. The devastating bush fires in 1967 destroyed four of these centres. Although there were fund raising efforts and the centre at Gardners Bay was rebuilt it was never sustainable again. Sam gives a glimpse into how these enormous changes have affected the Parish:

> Naturally, with the numbers dropping living in the town people attending the church numbers dropped quite dramatically. So finance, of course, became a problem and trying to keep a full-time rector did eventually become impossible. Different plans were thought out and parishes joined with neighbouring ones; for a short while with the Geeveston Parish which had gone into the same situation because the area was very similar to the Cygnet area so their problems were very similar to ours. Then later with the Huon and the Ranelagh Parish, they were all very difficult and seemed very hard to sustain and numbers seemed to continue to drop.
>
> I suppose at that stage it was probably a much more formal type of service and life than what it is now. At that stage we had a full-time rector and three services a Sunday. We'd have a quarter to 8 communion, family service at 11 o'clock and Evensong at 7. That went on for many, many years and then we had the outlying parishes. We had Gardners Bay, Lymington, Garden Island Creek, Nicholls Rivulet, and, on a monthly basis, they'd attend one of those in the afternoon which would be a 3 o'clock service. So it would be 3 o'clock the one Sunday at Gardners Bay and then Garden Island Creek, Lymington, taking in the four weeks in the month. (Sam, retired)

Prior to the Parish adopting ESM they found it impossible to sustain a full-time or even a part-time priest. At the main church centre at Cygnet, attendance had declined to about seven or eight people per week. As can be seen from the following comments, all the efforts of the Parish were focussed on fund raising and this had a negative impact on parishioners and the way the Parish was viewed by the wider community:

> I mean we did all sorts of fund-raising things, going around. There was an inter-denominational drive at one stage with Roman Catholics and, I think, Uniting Church people or Methodists as they were. We went round door-knocking and talking to people but where people would promise so much every so often it would just fall off after a while. They didn't keep their commitments up. Some people did but.... Yes. Always asking for money.... [and] door knocking just for money and I don't think that's right and it obviously didn't ring right with a lot of other people because they didn't give us masses of money and I don't think it [the church] should be open just for people to come and give money. (Louise, retired)

This on-going saga of money-raising by any means, as with the Parish of New Norfolk, became the sole focus of the Parish. For parishioners to go door-knocking for money is not only a sad reflection on the state of the Parish but also on the level of desperation experienced by these parishioners. As with so many rural communities of faith (or even urban ones) the emphasis on, and efforts in, raising money to pay for a stipendiary priest amounted to abject failure. And in Channel/Cygnet, there was a realization that the door-knocking ventures had actually been counter-productive in terms of the place and role of the church in the wider community, and the latter's view of the local Anglican Church.

One further unsuccessful Diocesan initiative was to amalgamate Cygnet and Channel (which has church centres at Woodbridge, Snug and Margate, though the centre at Margate is now in the process of being closed). The centres on the Channel are divided from Cygnet by a range of steep hills which form a physical, as well as a psychological, barrier between these communities and to drive from Cygnet to the Channel means negotiating this range and takes about half an hour to three quarters of an hour to drive between them (requiring the same amount of time on the return journey). Like almost all other amalgamations of parishes within the Diocese, this has not been successful, though Cygnet has tried very hard to sustain and develop a sustainable church life on the Channel. Harold comments on how difficult this challenge has been:

> It has been a huge challenge but I feel that the Parish has given it a very good shot, myself. People have put a lot of work, a lot of effort, a lot of thought, a lot of mission into the Channel. At this stage,

> unfortunately, I don't think we've been all that successful but I don't know that we can altogether blame ourselves. I think perhaps we've given it a fairly good shot. I don't think we're ready to give up quite yet but not quite sure what the future is there. (Harold, retired)

Despite a parish adopting ESM, or choosing to adopt ESM, there is still a need for a 'critical mass' of committed people so that the community of faith is able to be a sustainable church. Even then, sometimes things do not work out as planned, no matter how hard the efforts. 'Channel' continues to be difficult issue that the Parish of Channel/Cygnet still grapples with.

In the early days of the consultative period in Channel/Cygnet, during which time parishioners explored ESM as an option, some in the Parish felt that the Diocese were forcing them to adopt ESM, even though this far from the truth. The emphasis on allowing each parish to tell their story, walking with them, encouraging them to explore options, facilitating discussion, and emphasizing that each parish had the right and responsibility to make the final decision and that "whatever you decide is O.K.", even if it was closure or another option, was central to all Diocesan/parish discussions (Claude, priest). Nevertheless, dealing with change and difference, let alone embracing such things, is always difficult and frightening, and some parishioners in most parishes considering the option of ESM reacted with resistance, doubt, anxiety, or even anger.

In Channel/Cygnet, given the conservative nature of the Parish, there were particular issues to do with change management and theological/philosophical education concerning the paradigm shift from the traditional church model of stipendiary priest to ESM. As the following comments highlight, some of those within the Parish who felt ESM to be a 'second best' option largely did so on the basis of a conservative modelling of priestly ministry along with fixed views on music, worship, and dress 'norms':

> I know one lady who left … but there have been a couple of others who I think find it difficult. I don't know what it is. They find it difficult that it's still church and it's being led by people who are untrained. Even if they're doing training, it wasn't right in their view so they have decided to go to some other church. But I don't think Jesus had any degrees, so, I mean he had everything from God and he did what God told him but he didn't go to university or anything,

> or theology courses, or anything. But people didn't think that way. It's got to be... I don't know whether they just block their minds. I think that's what it is. They don't want to change, they don't want anything to be different. (Louise, retired)

The issues to do with resistance to change and attachment to 'old ways' are difficult to negotiate. In terms of the parishes choosing to look into ESM as a possibility, these issues were always undertaken with great care in relation to the specific local context and needs of the parishioners. Open and honest discussion and a willingness to address difficult issues were, and remain, primary characteristics of the ESM process.

Calling Out A Team

The Parish of Channel/Cygnet began exploring the possibility of ESM (or Total Ministry as it was initially called) in late 1999 and the first Local Ministry Support Team (LMST) was then formed. The Parish Council agreed to a date for a 'Calling Sunday' in May, 2001 to consider the calling of Team members and other parishioners to specific ministries within the Parish. This was seen as the last part of what was known as the 'Formation Stage' in the process of exploring ESM in Channel/Cygnet. The Parish was asked to prayerfully consider whom they believed should be called to the Team (whether they were currently Team members or not) and for which particular ministries (including Ordained Team Members). An outline of the qualities generally looked for in a Team member and in the specific areas of ministry to be called was provided to everyone in the Parish, along with the following information sheet:

> In the last year, our Parish has been journeying steadily towards Total Ministry [ESM]. We are now entering a very important period as we complete the Formation Stage of development.
>
> On Pentecost Sunday, 3 May [2001], members of all congregations in the Parish will have the opportunity to name the persons they believe are right to carry out various important leadership roles in the life of the Parish.
>
> The Parish Council and Local Ministry Support Team have agreed on the following leadership roles:
>
> - Ordained Team Members
> - Co-ordinator of Parish Administration

- Co-ordinator of Pastoral Care
- Co-ordinator of Outreach and Evangelism
- Co-ordinator of Children's, Youth and Family ministries

We hope to identify at least two people as Ordained Team Members in the Parish.

Oversight of the ministries of worship and prayer and teaching and discipleship will continue to be held corporately by the Ministry Support Team.

The people identified as being suitable for these leadership roles may, or may not, be members of the Ministry Support Team at this time. However, those who are called will be required to serve as members of the Team.

At the present time, the Team meets weekly, and the meeting usually lasts two hours. In addition, there are occasional training sessions. All members of the Team will participate in the Ministry Certificate Course which is due to start sometime soon after the Commissioning Service.

You are invited to spend time in reflection and prayer about who should be called to exercise these vital leadership roles in the life of the Parish. We are seeking people with the necessary qualities and gifts to exercise those ministries.

When a person is called to a specific ministry, it is not expected that they will be making a lifetime commitment to that ministry, except perhaps for those called to be Ordained Team Members. Every two to three years each role will be reviewed and a person may then stand down. When that happens someone will be called to replace them.

It is important to remember that the purpose of this process is **not** to reward or give recognition to those who have given faithful service to the church over the years though some of those who have done so may well prove to be gifted for these ministries.

A team of Visitors appointed by the Bishop will come to the Parish in July or early August to explore the readiness of the Parish and Team to take full responsibility for Parish ministry under the guidance of an Enabler. They will determine the suitability of the candidates named for Ordained ministry and make a recommendation to the Bishop for his prayerful consideration.

Once the Bishop has given his consent arrangements will be made to Commission the Parish and Team for Total Ministry. During the service those who have been called to serve as Priests will be ordained.

An outline of each leadership role and the qualities looked for in those who are to exercise it is set out on the following pages to help you in your prayerful reflection.

Remember that no one person will exhibit all the qualities and gifts listed below. What we want to do is to provide a firm basis for your reflection as you think about who is best fitted for each role.

1. 'Calling Sunday' and Formation

After the 'Calling Sunday', at which the 'nomination papers' (handed out a week or so before) were collected at the Offertory, the papers were taken by the Enabler for collation and prayerful deliberation. The Enabler, satisfied with the outcome expressed in the 'Calling' papers, then contacted each of the persons nominated to see whether they were happy to be recommended to the Bishop. The Enabler then discussed the outcome with the Diocesan Ministry Officer and the Bishop. After the Bishop had indicated his satisfaction and once the Enabler had checked that the candidates were still ready to proceed, the results were announced to the Parish.

The Enabler made it clear to the Parish that the new Team members were entering a period of formation as members of the Team and would be 'examined' by the Diocese to affirm their suitability for particular ministries (including Ordained Team Members) prior to their Commissioning and Ordination. The Vocational Advisors had some involvement in testing the calling of all candidates, especially those for Ordained Team Members. It was important to be sure that the Advisors used were people familiar with and supportive of ESM.

Generally, in parishes exploring ESM this period of formation is not intended to be too drawn out, maybe three months maximum (after all it is an apprenticeship model). Then there follows the service of Commissioning (of the whole Parish and of the Team) and Deaconing in the Parish context. Sometimes the Bishop may want the Deaconing as part of the stream of Ordinations in the Cathedral. Experience has taught that it is probably better to try and tie the Priesting in with the Diocesan Ordination timetable so that there is no question as to the validity of those Ordained as Priests. The Safe Ministry procedures automatically commenced for each of those called to membership of the Local Ministry Support Team at the appropriate time.

The following comments by Jane highlight how the whole Calling Out process is one that parishioners take very seriously:

> A Calling Out in some ways is a little bit like an election except that people aren't invited beforehand to nominate for various roles and parishioners are not given a list of names [of people] to vote for.... There is a period of prayer and discernment before the Calling Out where a specification, a description of the particular role that's being sought is circulated throughout the Parish so that all parishioners have an opportunity to reflect on the kind of person that's going to be needed for this role. They're given time; several weeks to reflect on it and pray about it and discuss it between themselves, if they want to. Then when the actual Calling Out takes place, which is usually after a Sunday morning service, people are invited to write the name or names of people who they feel are called or suitable for that role. It's really then, I think, a matter of the person who comes out clearly as being most widely called is approached by the Enabler to ask if they too feel that calling and if they're willing to accept the role. (Jane, artist)

2. Local Ministry Support Team

The sustainability of ESM as a way of being church depends, to a large extent, on finding suitable people to fulfil the demanding role of sharing the incumbency of the parish as a member of the Local Ministry Support Team. In some parishes, whether rural or urban, this is not possible, such as in the parishes of Southern Midlands or Moonah. The on-going sustainability of the parish requires that there be a depth of people in the parish so that there is a range of people with various gifts, skills, abilities, and strengths. In addition, this also allows for times when a member of the LMST needs to take time out or to step back. Other people can then be called by the parish to become members of the Local Ministry Support Team if and when required to do so. It is noteworthy of the flexibility afforded by the ESM model that the Channel Cygnet LMST and Parish have continued to flourish over the last nine years despite repeatedly losing key Team members, mostly from these people moving interstate, and also despite great personal tragedy affecting one of the LMST members and therefore the whole Parish.

ESM, therefore, fosters repeated callings-out when these are required. Hence, the process of second generation, third generation, fourth generation, and so on, callings-out become a part of the on-going life of the parish, as can be seen from the following outline of events at Channel/Cygnet:

14th September 2003: Calling Out for a new Co-ordinator of Administration as Bob Aitken had indicated that he intended to withdraw from the Team. Martin Hunnybun Called Out.

15th February 2004: Martin Hunnybun Commissioned as Co-ordinator of Administration and as a member of the Local Ministry Support Team at the annual Parish Weekend.

26th September 2004: Calling Out for a new Co-ordinator of Pastoral Care as John Middleton was no longer able to continue in that role and a new Co-ordinator of Children's Ministry as Terry Robson was no longer able to continue in that role. Marg Gordon was Called Out to be the new Co-ordinator of Pastoral Care, but not a Team member. Tracey Salmon was Called Out to be the new Co-ordinator of Children's Ministry and as a member of the Local Ministry Support Team.

17th October 2004: Marg Gordon was Commissioned as the new Co-ordinator of Pastoral Care, but not a Team member. Tracey Salmon was Commissioned as the new Co-ordinator of Children's Ministry and as a member of the Local Ministry Support Team.

17th October 2004: Eleanor O'Donnell withdraws from the Local Ministry Support Team as she has been appointed and Commissioned as the Chaplain at St Michael's Collegiate School. The Reverend Martin Hunnybun, in consultation with the Team, agrees to assist with Priestly Ministry within the Parish due to Eleanor's withdrawal from the Team (though Eleanor agreed to assist in the Parish with Priestly Ministry when she was able to do so).

Again, this process of having repeated callings-out when necessary enables each ESM parish to be able to sustain the level of shared leadership required by the Local Ministry Support Team (as the shared incumbent of the parish). In this way, the mission and ministry of the Parish can be carried out without undue pressure being placed on one person, or several people, and with the facility to call out new people when needed. Within each of the parishes examined in the case studies, this process has become an integral part of their on-going life.

Those called to membership of the Local Ministry Support Team share the incumbency of the parish and hence the Calling Out process is always scrutinized at a Diocesan level. This is the same process for discerning the calling of any person to incumbency of a parish within the Diocese; so it is not a matter of just trying to get someone to fill a vacant position but of discerning if the person called out is really suitable for the demanding role to which they have been called. Some people have declined the offer to serve as members of the Local Ministry Support Team. Others have requested that their membership be delayed until they have some more space in their life. In Rev Collins' experience, however, there has never been an instance of expediently filling a role on the LMST just for the sake of it or just to make up numbers.

Furthermore, the focus on Team ministry and the participation of all members in the community of faith in the decision making process is something that resonates with the post-modern paradigm. In this paradigm, as Drane (2001) comments, there is an emphasis on learning that arises from mutual discussion and guided experience and there is a preference for decisions that arise from the consensus of the group rather than from policy or instruction manuals. Tomlinson (1995) and Frost (2006) echo similar opinions that stress collaborative learning and management in communities of faith.

Within the Parish of Channel/Cygnet, there has now been a universal acceptance of ESM and the negative scrutiny of the Team that was in evidence from some quarters in the early days has diminished. The Team never rejected other voices, even critical and negative ones, and sought to dialogue with all in the Parish. In the process of becoming an ESM parish the parishioners began to take a greater responsibility for the life of the Parish. Some parishioners have found the introduction of a new way of being church to be exciting. Others have found the change more difficult because members of the parish were 'up-front' leading services, praying, preaching, and presiding at the Eucharist. As the following quote from Louise highlights, achieving the sustainable life within the Parish that ESM fostered required many parishioners to step out of their 'comfort-zones':

> Very nerve-wracking to begin with. Very nerve-wracking. To have been in the congregation all my life and never... I hated even doing Bible readings which I think I started on before I led services but I hated getting up and reading in front of people or have been embarrassed about reading. Leading, again, was very embarrassing and very daunting to face the congregation instead of being part of it, but I've got more used to it now and a lot of people have encouraged me and I feel that it's part of playing my part in our church and I'm helping others to have a service, so I quite enjoy it I suppose now. My knees knock occasionally. (Louise, retired)

This is an engagement with change as opposed to a resistance to change. Nevertheless, the former can be frightening, both to the congregation and to the person fulfilling a ministry role in front of the congregation. Once people experienced the quality and care of all involved, especially from those on the Local Ministry Support Team, any difficulties evaporated. Only one person left the Parish because of the introduction of ESM. As Sue comments below, a new attitude of care for all people (within the Parish and without) and encouragement to support one another meant that people were prepared to create a sustainable future for the Parish by helping in all aspects of parish life and by becoming more involved in the wider community, too:

> Well, probably the most ... the clearest one for me is the life that it's brought to the Parish. It seems that with the recognition that ordinary people can do this magic ministry thing that we all talk so much about, that it's actually given permission to a whole lot of other people to do all kinds of things and to be enthusiastic about things. Despite all that I've said about non-stipendiary ministry and all the rest of it, people are very aware, within the Parish, of the time that people give, whether they're on the Team or not and are becoming much more inclined to notice and thank people for the things that they do rather than thinking, oh well, that's their job and they get paid to do it so we won't even notice. So there's a lot more of that, a lot more looking out for people. People ringing each other up and making sure they're okay and getting involved. (Sue, teacher)

ESM in Practice

Parishioners see the strength of ESM as being the freedom it gives for people to own the life of the parish and the living out of their faith in all parts of their life. This might involve visiting elderly or sick people. An example of this is the group run by the Parish called 'Eating with Friends'. This group provides meals and social contact for those in the wider community who are unable to ever eat out or who might not prepare suitably nutritious meals for themselves. Other out-reach examples include visiting at the hospital, providing meals to those in need, helping clean and repair homes of people who are not able to look after them by themselves, study groups, prayer groups, supporting the Chaplain at Woodbridge High School, re-furbishing the Parish hall for use by the whole community, and pastoral care of any and all within the community. Sam's comment below highlights the collaborative spirit and initiative that ESM has encouraged in parishioners in the Channel/Cygnet Parish:

> I think it's the input; it's people's willingness to share and to work together and really, I think, this is the whole key to Ministry Support [ESM]. Instead of sitting back and trying to raise finance to keep a full-time rector, people out there doing what they want to do, and they're getting the satisfaction and the rewards for the effort that they're putting in and I think that grows. Well, I know it grows because I've seen it happen and where we see one success then another one seems to come along much easier. We've got people willing to stand up and say, well this is what I would like to see happen and they do something about it. This is how I think the wonderful thing with Enabler Supported Ministry, people are achieving what they want to see in their Parish and they're doing it with their time, with their effort and with other people's help and support. (Sam, retired)

There was a marked change in the Parish of Channel/Cygnet, as with the New Norfolk Parish, from a focus on raising funds to pay the priest's stipend to out-reach activities in the wider community. The financial commitment by the Parish to support the Chaplain at Woodbridge High School, to renovate the Parish hall (so that it can be used by the whole community), and to support community activities indicates this change within the Parish that ESM facilitated. As Louise suggests, this also indicates a change in attitude in the Parish from looking in to looking out:

> I think it's part of the wider community. I still think that we still have to get out or do things outside 'The Church' more but sometimes it's very hard to think what. We have supported a Chaplain going into a school in the Parish, at Woodbridge. At Snug the retirement village is having services held there and visits being made there. I think we're gradually doing more but sometimes it's difficult to know where else you can go and proclaim the gospel, so to speak. I think all of us still have a reticence about climbing on a soap box and just standing there and spouting, like at Hyde Park. (Louise, retired)

It is worth commenting that the financial commitment by the Parish to support the Chaplain at Woodbridge High School does not immediately benefit the community of faith at Cygnet. That is, this is a gift given by the Parish to benefit the community on the Channel. Although the Channel is part of the Parish of Channel/Cygnet, the vast majority of the Parish is made up of people from the Cygnet area.

The Commissioning of the Parish and the Local Ministry Support Team in 2002 was held in the Cygnet Town Hall because of the large number of people attending. This re-location was an issue for several people. Two key parishioners, as well as one other former parishioner who had already left the Parish, did not attend this service because of it being held in the Town Hall. However, as can be seen from the following quote, these two are now among the strongest supporters of what is happening in the Parish:

> One in particular we lost altogether and I know that was purely because of ESM. She wasn't happy but, fortunately, she's found a place to worship where she is happy.... I think, when we had the ordinations it was such a big occasion that we weren't able to fit it into the church so it was moved into the Town Hall. A couple of our really strong stalwarts in the church wouldn't attend because it wasn't a consecrated area. That was their objection. Now they are probably some of our strongest supporters and are working, with all of us, very, very hard. (Harold, retired)

An objection or a criticism of the ESM model that is often raised is the danger that could arise from the presence of people with strong and overbearing personalities. It is possible that strong personalities could have an undue influence on the Team but this situation has been avoided here, as with the Teams in the other three Parishes examined in the case studies, because the Team work through all issues together, even the difficult issues. Ammerman (2001) makes the point that a healthy church depends on parishioners working through any difficult issues. ESM is a model of church where all are encouraged to participate in the life of the parish. The Team, along with the Enabler (who acts as a consultant to the Team), encourage others to be involved in the Parish and its activities. Louise's comments below highlight how the benefit of a Team ministry is that it ensures the needs of all parishioners are being met by offering to parishioners a variety of contact points with people who are caring:

> I think the Team have been very humble and have been solid together. I think they have tried to always get people if they have any problem at all to approach somebody on the Team and because it's a Team it's not one person. I mean some people are difficult to approach. Some people are easier for different people to approach but they've all been very, I think, kind and humble and human and easy to approach for different people. I don't know if you know what I'm getting at? I mean not everybody's the same so one person might find it was easier to go to one person than the other three or four or whatever. I think the Team has made themselves very approachable by their attitude; not built themselves up into places of power and I think they have won over, by their attitude and their actions, all the people that perhaps had rather negative feelings about it all. (Louise, retired)

The issues of concern for some parishioners about becoming an ESM parish and, in particular, having a Team included apprehension that there might be a lack of focus in not having one person as the incumbent (that is, the rector) as there was a Team and all parishioners were becoming involved. For others it was anxiety about power (parishioners who were now perceived to have it), and for others it was a concern about confidentiality (speaking to 'another' parishioner instead of to the rector). Whereas, the benefits of ESM actually included unlocking the latent energy of the gifts of the whole Parish as all people are involved. The whole Parish now owns being an ESM parish, even those who had serious reservations to begin with. As Harold observes, any reservations against the LMST, or ESM generally, disappeared during the development of ESM in the parish:

> I think once people became aware of their ministry and experienced their ministry within the church that those faded away very quickly

> and they became very much accepted and very responsible and very loving and caring and I think, well, I know, that they're very, very highly thought of; very, very highly respected. We would find it very difficult now to do without them; they're fantastic. (Harold, retired)

In the Parish of Channel/Cygnet, as with the other parishes, those 'called out' represented the community of faith as well as the demographic make-up of the wider community. At Channel/Cygnet, this resulted in new-comers to the area being 'called out' to serve on the Team. There was no one called out who had been born in the district. The composition of the Team has changed over the years and yet the make-up of the Team remains similar in that it consists of those who have moved into the town or district more recently. This probably reflects the continuing migration of people into the area, particularly 'tree-changers', 'alternative life-stylers', and others who find the district an attractive place in which to live

The Parish, despite claims that it would fall apart under ESM, has now enjoyed the greatest period of stability in its recent history. The Channel/Cygnet Parish has now been Commissioned as an ESM parish for almost a decade. The change of focus from fund raising to ministry has meant that the Parish has been able to engage with the community. As Sam's comments below indicate, the Parish owns its own life and the wider community is recognizing, resonating with, and affirming the life within the Parish:

> Well, I think it's the opportunity for people to use their gifts to contribute to their religious life in the community; to offer the community their gifts and to be out there living their religion and not just going to church on Sunday and calling ourselves Anglicans. I think we're out there as living, working, enjoying being Anglicans. (Sam, retired)

The social make-up of the district includes a diverse range of life-styles and backgrounds and, as Sally observes, the wider community has embraced the church doing something that has a local focus and is 'home grown':

> I think that a really, really important thing in all of that is that the wider community knows that there is no priest in charge. They also know that the church is probably more alive than it has been for years and is becoming aware of the various ones who are on the Team and the other things that they do with their lives and so I think our connections in the local community are still strengthened

> considerably. And I have found it interesting, in terms of acceptance of local people whether lay or ordained doing various ministry tasks, that it was the local community beyond the church that was far more accepting and enthusiastic about that in the early stages than the church itself. (Sally, student)

The Parish has a significant pastoral ministry and this pastoral ministry includes many people from the church being involved, not only members of the LMST. Fred's comments indicate that there is an awareness amongst those in the wider community that the Parish has a concern for, and support of, social justice issues:

> There's an awareness amongst the community who are associated with social justice issues that the church exists and has an ear for such issues and even though it might not be the first place they come to attempt to redress some of the problems in our society, nonetheless they are appreciative of the support of the church, that part of the church which resonates with [them]. (Fred, farmer)

Other cultural/community activities include Anzac Day and the support of refugees. In particular, the members of the Parish support Rwandan refugees in a practical way and advocate for their needs at a political level (local, state and federal), and give emotional/spiritual support, too. This is an amazing expression of outward care to a level that would have been thought completely impossible a decade earlier when Parish numbers had dwindled to a very low level and the focus was on raising funds to pay the stipend. As Fred explains, a need was recognized and the Parish responded:

> The Rwandans who live in Hobart at the moment, there are only two families, 13 individuals I've come to know personally through introduction and become quite good friends with them and became aware of their cultural isolation and their separation from family members and associates who are refugees or residents in Rwanda or neighbouring countries who are living a tenuous existence and sometimes more dangerous than that and so we initiated ... we basically formed a vehicle by which refugees could be sponsored into Australia which was basically under the church umbrella with involvement of a number of church members. So we've been raising funds and we've been putting in applications for visas. We've got about

> half a dozen underway and … recognised as being in the pipeline and we've been lobbying the politicians.
>
> We've been at considerable effort to awaken community awareness about the plight of Rwandans in Hobart as well as those refugees who are in neighbouring countries and … still in Rwanda. So we are also looking towards attempting to have the Australian Government make some changes in immigration policy and hopefully to use some influence to practically redress some of the problems … in Rwanda which are accentuating the problems which flow from genocide. Things, for example, where some 80,000 odd Hutu prisoners are still awaiting trial from genocide which happened 11 years ago. This creates enormous resentment not only amongst that population but also in their families and in their communities and whilst there are militant Hutus who are, again, activating to reignite the genocide and continue to try and finish that genocide exercise off, the environment in Rwanda is becoming that much more dangerous and tense. So, it really needs international intervention, the kind of actions which should have taken place which are outside the scope of the Rwandan Government to implement which really needs international assistance and involvement…. We're just attempting to bring some of those matters to light and see if we can get a snowball started. (Fred, farmer)

That a rural parish almost on the verge of closure has so managed to re-invent itself as to be lobbying politicians and sponsoring Rwandan refugees is a staggering achievement. While this entirely stems from the parishioners themselves in the living out of their Christian faith, it is the ESM model of church that has facilitated this. This Parish project is widely supported in the Cygnet area. One of the fund-raising ventures started by one of the LMST members is the Rwandan Coffee Club, which imports coffee and tea from Rwanda or other developing nations for sale in Australia. All proceeds go to support Rwandan refugees in Australia and projects in Rwanda that benefit genocide survivors. There is also a website that explains about the plight of the Rwandans, sells the coffee and tea on-line, and encourages support and assistance for Rwandans (*Rwandan Coffee Club*). This is a rather poignant and beautiful example of how ESM works.

The Channel/Cygnet Parish also connects with the community on environmental issues. For example, the Parish helped to organize the 'Liturgy in the Forest' which was held in the Styx Valley on Sunday the 17th of November, 2002. Other Christian groups and environmentalists were also involved. Though the liturgy was focused on a Christian concern for the preservation of creation, as Fred makes clear, it was framed in such a way that people of any faith or none could participate:

> We certainly had a strong feeling of harmony between a lot of the local community with the involvement we had in conducting the Liturgy in the Forest a few years ago and so a lot of the local community related very strongly to that who were environmentally minded and so it's issues like these which have, as I say, helped the local community realize that the church has an ear for their concerns. (Fred, farmer)

ESM has affirmed and recognized the place of women within the Parish. Women are represented at every level of leadership within the Parish (as in each of the four ESM parishes examined in the case studies), including the Team's role as shared incumbent. Fred makes the point that often the issue is whether people know the priest not what gender the priest is and

> by and large I'm sure that the female leadership that's been exercised in our congregation has been almost universally appreciated with there being no gender differentiation. In the community at large I think that there may be some people who still carry some stereotypical perceptions and when the question comes up, for example, as to whether they prefer to have a male or female priest conduct a funeral then it is much more relevant as to whether they know the female priest or the male priest as to their choice, rather than making a decision of stereotypes. (Fred, farmer)

Parishioners are very hopeful about the future of the Parish, even though there have been some people who have left the Parish over the years (due mainly to them requiring access to medical care). There are always others who take on leadership roles, when people have left, and there is no sense that this will not continue. There is a sense of optimism and enthusiasm in the Parish. Attendance is now between 40 and 60 on any Sunday. Parishioners are thrilled at how well church services are now attended compared to how it was in the late 1990's:

> We've seen a really fantastic turnaround. To me it's been wonderful. It's almost gone back to when we used to attend church as kids as a family and we're now seeing those family groups returning and it's quite a thrill to me to walk in and see Mum and Dad and three or four children, which was commonplace when I was young. So, it's fantastic to see that come back. (Harold, retired)

Conclusion

The story of the transformation that has occurred to the Parish of Channel/Cygnet, as with the story of the Parish of New Norfolk in the preceding chapter, is one that speaks of hope. It is also a story that speaks about embracing change and embracing difference. Moreover, it is a story that has value not only in its telling, but also in interpreting it and making it available to others.

Parishes that are struggling financially invariably become inward looking. Although this is not the intention, this inward-looking stance happens because parishioners are trying to raise funds. Clinging on to the model of a full-time stipendiary priest when it is clearly not leading to a healthy parish community or a sustainable future inadvertently leads to an inward-looking focus. Making a change to ESM, however, frees the parish up, but also maintains accountability and training, and transforms the inward-looking focus to an outward-looking focus. Most importantly, ESM enables a strong relational model of being church that facilitates the Parish's engagement with and support of the wider community. This model, and the engagement it enables, is both theologically grounded in Anglican belief and sociologically grounded in the social and cultural context of the community of faith.

In the Parish of Channel/Cygnet, ESM has led to a sustainable future for the community of faith because it changes the way that parishioners relate to each other – they keep in contact more and care for each other. However, this is only one aspect of the success of ESM. The parishioners at Channel/Cygnet have moved from an inward focus to an outward focus of caring for all in their community, as well as participating in the global struggles that they see on their televisions, as in their support of Rwandan refugees and in their participation in environmental issues. This movement has also resulted in a greater connection and respect *for* the wider community by the faith community, and also *by* the wider community for the faith community.

Consistent with the discussion of the ideas of various theorists in Chapter One, the community of faith at Channel/Cygnet is characterized neither by "insipidness" (Berger 1992: 180) nor by "unbelievable fanaticism" (Berger 1992: 180). Rather, through the 'elective affinity' facilitated by ESM between the cultural context of the group (the faith position of this Anglican parish) and their social context the Parish is now characterized by a rich outward expression of their faith through engagement and care. This community of faith has become an example of what Ammerman (2001), Bouma (2006) and Cray (2007) describe as the enrichment of the wider community by the local church.

Indeed, the nature of the radical change in the Parish of Channel/Cygnet that ESM has fostered can be seen in the change from a situation of door-knocking to raise money to keep going as a parish to a very different situation of raising money to sponsor and support refugees and genocide victims. This is a cameo portrait of 'elective affinity' in action, where ESM, as a different way of being church, has facilitated a synergy between action and reflection. As an example of an inductive, sociologically informed theological orientation ESM promotes engagement with the wider community, which in turn facilitates a reciprocity of engagement and mutual enrichment, respect, and collaboration. The choice of an ethnographic approach to the research allows for the telling of the extraordinary stories of these ordinary and typical Tasmanian rural parishes, but also 'an' interpretation of them and why they are so full of hope, and finally a sharing of these stories.

A Chronology of Events

1997: Parish of Cygnet amalgamated with Channel (minus Bruny Island) to form Parish of Channel/Cygnet.

1998: the Diocese appoints a priest (Claude) as the Diocesan Ministry Officer (1998-2002).

Early 1998: last Rector appointed (full-time) to Parish.

June 1999: Rector's appointment reduced to part-time.

20th – 21st November 1999: Parish weekend held. Team members from the Parish of New Norfolk came and spoke about Enabler Supported Ministry.

3rd May 2000: a Local Ministry Support Team formed and begins to meet fortnightly.

February 2001: last Rector leaves Parish.

June 2001: Team members 'Called Out' to specific ministries

Co-ordinator of Pastoral Care – John Middleton

Co-ordinator of Administration – Bob Aitken

Co-ordinator of Outreach – Ann Martin

Co-ordinator of Children's Ministry – Terry Robson

Locally Ordained Ministry – Eleanor O'Donnell & John Middleton.

July 2001: Diocesan visitation to Parish to determine whether the Parish was ready to be Commissioned (the visiting team included the Reverend Neil Vearing, the Reverend Sharon Green and Dr David Thomas).

August 2001: Ordination candidates interviewed by the Bishop.

30th August 2001: Ordination to the Diaconate of 10 people Called to Ordained ministry from five parishes (Channel/Cygnet, New Norfolk, St Helens, Circular Head, Sheffield).

1st September 2001: James Collins begins as Enabler to parishes of Channel/Cygnet, New Norfolk and St Helens.

3rd October 2001: James Collins Commissioned as Enabler to parishes of Channel/Cygnet, New Norfolk and St Helens.

15th February 2002: Full Commissioning of Parish of Channel/Cygnet including the Commissioning of the Local Ministry Support Team (John Middleton, Bob Aitken, Ann Martin, Terry Robson, Eleanor O'Donnell and Michael Groth) and the Ordination to the Priesthood of those Called to Ordained ministry in the Parish (Eleanor O'Donnell & John Middleton).

February 2002: Parish Weekend held to celebrate Commissioning of the Parish.

May 2002: The Diocesan Ministry Officer (Claude) leaves the Diocese.

14th September 2003: Calling Out for a new Co-ordinator of Administration as Bob Aitken had indicated that he intended to withdraw from the Team. Martin Hunnybun Called Out.

15th February 2004: Martin Hunnybun Commissioned as Co-ordinator of Administration and as a member of the Local Ministry Support Team at the annual Parish Weekend.

26th September 2004: Calling Out for a new Co-ordinator of Pastoral Care as John Middleton was no longer able to continue in that role and a new Co-ordinator of Children's Ministry as Terry Robson was no longer able to continue in that role. Marg Gordon was Called Out to be the new Co-ordinator of Pastoral Care, but not a Team member. Tracey Salmon was Called Out to be the new Co-ordinator of Children's Ministry and as a member of the Local Ministry Support Team.

17th October 2004: Marg Gordon was Commissioned as the new Co-ordinator of Pastoral Care, but not a Team member. Tracey Salmon was Commissioned as the new Co-ordinator of Children's Ministry and as a member of the Local Ministry Support Team.

17th October 2004: Eleanor O'Donnell withdraws from the Local Ministry Support Team as she has been appointed and Commissioned as the Chaplain at St Michael's Collegiate School. The Reverend Martin Hunnybun, in consultation with the Team, agrees to assist with Priestly Ministry within the Parish due to Eleanor's withdrawal from the Team (though Eleanor agreed to assist in the Parish with Priestly Ministry when she was able to do so).

28th February 2007: James Collins resigns as Enabler to the Parish of Channel/Cygnet and Helen Phillips is appointed as the Enabler.

Chapter Four: The Parish of St Helens (Break O'Day)

Introduction

This chapter describes how the introduction of Enabler Supported Ministry to the Parish of St Helens (now known as Break O'Day) led to a reversal of what had been an on-going story of parish decline for several decades. It outlines how the process of change at St Helens reflects the way that this process of change manifests in various parish contexts throughout the Diocese and how ESM allows for parishes to engage with this on-going change. With particular reference to St Helens, the chapter examines how social changes led to the Parish beginning a furniture ministry to address the emerging issues of poverty in the area. Becoming an ESM parish has allowed a previously conservative parish that was against women's ministry to accept and affirm the role of women within the Parish, reflecting broader cultural changes within society.

Background

St Helens, in Tasmanian terms, is an isolated community on the East coast of the State, and was primarily a traditional fishing port. During the mid-1970's the fishing industry collapsed in the town due to the advent of larger and better-equipped vessels fishing in the area. These fishing boats generally had their 'home' ports located elsewhere in the State or on the Australian mainland. It is only in recent years that the town of St Helens, and the surrounding district, has attracted a large influx of 'sea-changers' (and 'tree changers' in St Marys).

Rev James Collins drove to St Helens once per month and stayed from the Friday through to the Sunday and spent time with the Team and others in the Parish to train, supervise, and mentor them. This arrangement of an intensive visit once per month worked well due to the relative isolation of the Parish, particularly from Hobart, which is where he lives.

Rev Collins usually drove north along the Midlands Highway. This route takes him through two other large rural parishes which have almost ceased to function. The Parish of Southern Midlands has a large number of centres and begins just north of Brighton and extends to Tunbridge, the unofficial divide between the north and south of the State. The Parish of Northern Midlands then begins and extends along the Fingal Valley to Fingal, taking in Ross and Campbell Town, and even took in Cressy for a while. Each of these centres used to be a parish in its own right. Their demise as separate parishes reflects the Diocesan policy of amalgamating parishes. This policy has proved to be a very poor response to the issues faced by rural parishes.

As individual parishes begin to struggle to pay the priest's stipend (the measure of viability in this traditional stipendiary model being attendance numbers and financial giving) one struggling parish is amalgamated with another struggling parish. The result of this amalgamation process is that one person, the rector, is spread over two parishes trying to provide pastoral care, officiate at worship services, maintain the life of the two former separate parishes, and is spread even thinner as more and more parishes are amalgamated.

This policy of amalgamation has not worked anywhere in Tasmania and the Diocese is littered with large multi-centre parishes which have, over time, been amalgamated and then amalgamated again and then amalgamated again. The Parish of Southern Midlands now has eleven centres (thirteen centres if two centres which have been leased out to community groups are counted) and the Parish of Northern Midlands now has five centres (and grew to nine centres at one stage when it took in the Parish of Cressy).

The problem with parishes getting too big geographically is that they can no longer be amalgamated with any other neighbouring parishes. The emphasis on sustaining a stipend for the rector proves to be impossible and then the rector's appointment is made fractional. That is, one person is expected to do all the work that probably three to five (or more) other people did when each parish was autonomous before all of the amalgamations took place; and now the one person is expected to do all of this on a half-time basis. This is clearly an untenable situation for both rector and parishes, and eventually even a part-time appointment cannot be financially sustained.

Once the fractional appointment can no longer be supported then often an honorary priest is appointed to do all of the work for no stipend (with maybe free accommodation in the Rectory and travel costs covered). Another option is that of 'supply priests' who come on an *ad hoc* basis. Meanwhile, any on-going life in the parish has ground to a halt because the focus on sustaining the priest's stipend and paying the bills became the sole focus of the parish and fund-raising consumed all of the time and energy of the parishioners (how many lamington drives can one small rural town cope with?). This is not a tirade against these parishes or a negative comment on what has eventuated in these parishes. Rather, it is a recognition that sustaining the rector model in a context of social and cultural change has serious and long-term consequences that, if not addressed, can result in distress, anger, and despair for faithful parishioners and often eventual closure or further amalgamation of parishes.

Sometimes Rev Collins drove north along the East Coast of Tasmania to get to St Helens. Along this route, he drove through three other rural parishes that have similar histories to the parishes of Southern and Northern Midlands. The Parish of Sorell, Richmond and Tasman has seven centres from Colebrook to Port Arthur. The Parish of Buckland has five centres from Buckland to Triabunna. The Parish of Swansea/Bicheno is unique in only having two centres, but the Parish is a co-operating parish between the Anglican and Uniting Churches. They combined forces due to the same financial pressures that have impacted on each of the other parishes mentioned already. This so called 'co-operating' Parish has been marked by a lack of co-operation between the Anglican and Uniting Church parishioners and has experienced periods of almost total dysfunction with each group maintaining their separate identity and never combining for worship services. Fortunately, however, this situation has recently improved, breathing some new life into this Parish.

This repertoire of responses to the issues faced by rural parishes, which tend to comprise amalgamations, fractional appointments, honorary appointments, supply priests, and co-operation with other denominations, have all proved to be minimally successful, if not totally unsuccessful, in maintaining any sustainable life within any of the parishes. This research helps explore this issue: an issue that is a dilemma for the Diocese and a source of pain and anguish for the affected parishioners. The research explores from a sociological perspective how such parishes can have a sustainable future. This sociological perspective is thus not only insightful but also allows for an exploration of issues 'outside' the Church that are also very much issues 'inside' the Church because no parish exists in 'splendid isolation' as it is affected by social and cultural context within contemporary society.

St Helens: A Description of the Town and Region (Break O'Day Municipality)

The Break O'Day municipality is bounded by the Dorset, Northern Midlands, and Launceston municipalities. This rural municipality has some remote areas that can be difficult to access. The geographical features of the municipality have influenced the population distribution and access to services.

As one approaches St Helens from St Marys, coming along the Fingal Valley, the descent from the highlands along the valley down to the coastal plain is an impressive and, sometimes, dangerous drive. There are two routes where the descent from the highlands to the plain can occur. St Marys Pass heads in a north-east direction whilst Elephant Pass heads in an east-north-east direction. Both roads are narrow and winding and afford spectacular views to the coastal plain and ocean beyond.

The East Coast from St Helens to Bicheno is a significant holiday area, particularly during the summer months; although increasing numbers of people are choosing to move to the area either to live and work with their family or to retire. St Helens is the largest town on the East Coast of Tasmania and, like most other East Coast towns, was centred around the fishing industry as the following quote from Graham indicates:

> Well, when we arrived it was a very busy port. Something like 40 boats registered out of this port and now it's probably less than ten. We have Victorian boats coming in to unload but they're not registered and so the families aren't living near the infrastructure that supports the industry; gone. But then we've had things like the mussels and the oysters have started up but not to the [same] extent. (Graham, business proprietor)

St Helens is approximately 2 hours' drive to Launceston and 3 hours to Hobart. A district hospital is located in St Helens, as are a number of community and health services. St Marys is located approximately 35 kilometres inland from St Helens. The two passes mentioned above divide the two towns and these sections of road represent a psychological and geographical barrier for people. For financial reasons the State Government closed the acute care services provided at St Marys District Hospital in October 1997. This facility is now developing into a community health centre.

The Break O'Day Municipality comprises some 3,809 square kilometres (Australian Bureau of Statistics 1996). The 1996 Census of Population and

Housing (Australian Bureau of Statistics 1996) counted 459,659 people in Tasmania on census night. The total number of people living in Northern Tasmania is 131,764, which is approximately 29% of the total population. The Break O'Day Municipality has a population 5,644 (Australian Bureau of Statistics 1996). There were slightly more females than males counted in Tasmania on census night (50.8% and 49.2% of the total Tasmanian population, respectively). However, in the Break O'Day municipality there were 2,858 males and 2,786 females (Australian Bureau of Statistics 1996), which might reflect the rural setting of the region having a predominantly male workforce (fishing, forestry, farming).

The highest median ages were recorded in the North Eastern Statistical Subdivision, of which St Helens (Break O'Day) forms a part, which was 37 years. This area also recorded a high percentage of people aged 65 years and over (14.1%), indicating a relatively old age profile. This may reflect the areas' recent popularity as a retirement destination. Many of the outlying Statistical Local Areas recorded the highest median ages, including Break O'Day (38 years). Break O'Day also recorded a high proportion of people aged 65 years and over (14.8%).

The Anglican Parish of St Helens – A Description

1. Decline and the Journey Towards ESM

The Parish of St Helens has recently changed its name to the Parish of Break O'Day (2007), as this is the name of the municipality. The name change of the Parish also reflects the former amalgamation of the Parish with the Parish of St Marys. The Parish also takes in Pyengana. Other centres used to be located at Gould's County, Falmouth, Gray, Cullenswood, and Cornwall but these have all been closed, given away, or have fallen down (Centenary Committee of St. Paul's Church, St. Helens 1983).

From 1990 to 1993, the then incumbent of the Parish was ill, often unable to work and frequently off on sick leave. Two Lay Readers worked to maintain worship and pastoral care within the Parish. This situation continued during a very long inter-regnum and when the next Rector was appointed it became increasingly clear that the Parish could no longer afford to sustain a full-time stipendiary ministry. From 1996 to 2000, the last Rector, recognizing that the Parish could not sustain a stipend, developed lay ministry even further within the Parish as the following quote from Elizabeth indicates:

> Well, with the decline in population and that was along with the rest of rural Australia at the time, we couldn't sustain his stipend, basically. We were running close to having no money. So he, well, really helped us make the decision by saying, you can do it yourselves and by him resigning we were forced. If you want ministry to continue somebody's got to do it. How we do that and in what way ... but I think we'd grown strong enough to know that we could do it. (Elizabeth, teacher)

Given the inability to afford a full-time stipendiary priest (and the unlikelihood of even affording or attracting a part-time appointment) the Parish recognized that, if it was to continue, a new way of being church was required. At that time, the Diocese employed a priest as the Diocesan Ministry Officer (1998-2002), who recognized that many parishes were facing similar problems to those at St Helens, including New Norfolk, Channel/Cygnet, and Hamilton. Therefore, another way of being church was required. Over time he developed what came to be known as Enabler Supported Ministry (ESM), which began as Collaborative Ministry, was then called Total Ministry, and finally became ESM.

The Diocesan Ministry Officer visited the Parish of St Helens as often as possible and held numerous discussions with the Parish. As Barbara's comments indicate, the Parish realized early on that ESM was worth exploring and implementing:

> From what I believe from the other members … they had no way of having a full time priest as a rector and they investigated [ESM] and decided it would be the best way for them to go for the Parish to survive. (Barbara, retired)

In October 1999, the Parish Council voted unanimously to pursue this new way of being church. In November 1999, the Parish began a 5-week 'Journey of Discovery' for developing this so called Collaborative Ministry. At the end of this 5-week journey, the Parish decided to continue exploring this new way of being church and appointed a steering committee. The Enabler's role was outlined, and in February 2000 there was a commitment to embark on an education programme. Another education programme commenced after the Ash Wednesday Service on the 8th of March 2000 exploring the nature of Local Collaborative Ministry as ESM was then called.

In June 2000, the Parish had a farewell for the Rector, who was their last stipendiary priest. Another workshop on ESM was held in July 2000 and then the Annual General Meeting was held in August 2000, where a unanimous decision was made in favour of the Parish becoming an ESM parish. October was set aside as a month of prayer and reflection, with the 'Calling Out' process set for the 29th of October. The Parish Council agreed on the following areas of ministry to which parishioners would be called so as to form a Local Ministry Support Team (LMST) for the Parish: teaching, administration, children's ministry, pastoral care, evangelism, prayer, and healing, as well as Locally Ordained Priests (now known as Ordained Team Members: OTM's). On Wednesday the 13th of December 2000 the Parish held a special service to mark the beginning of the Formation Stage of Development of ESM.

As with the make-up of those 'called out' in the other parishes, those 'called out' in the Parish of St Helens reflected the demographic make-up of the surrounding district: they were all new-comers to the area. While the composition of the Team has changed over the years in terms of individual members, the make-up of the Team has remained the same in that it comprises those who have moved into the area more recently. As with Channel/Cygnet, this probably reflects the fact that St Helen's has become a desirable place to live – in this case for the 'sea-changers'.

There were some initial problems with the introduction of Enabler Supported Ministry, as there were in the other parishes I examined. However, as the following comments from Tom indicate, these problems were dealt with openly and time was taken to ensure that anyone with a concern was able to voice their concern and have it addressed:

> I think at the beginning we had a lot of negatives, especially with our older members … This [ESM] was completely new and they weren't very happy about it. It was a matter of just talking to them and talking through those negatives and I think we visited just about every elderly person in the Parish and sat down and asked them their problems and then talked through their problems. It took a long time because these talks would probably last an hour or two.
>
> And whenever we got the opportunity, we would talk to our members about the situation. How it was going to, we hoped, be done. It sounds like I was very much for Enabler Supported Ministry back then … and I must admit I was. I could see that in the past the Parish Council, yeah, it was the governing body of the Parish but really, when it all boiled down, it used to just rubber stamp what the rector wanted.

This way, the Parish Council were going to be accountable for what they decided. They had to make the decisions. (Tom, retired)

2. The Change to Enabler Supported Ministry

On Ash Wednesday, the 13th of February, 2002, the Portland Memorial Hall in St Helens was packed with some 250 local people to witness and participate in the service to mark the official launch of Enabler Supported Ministry in the Parish of St Helens, including the Commissioning of parishioners, the Commissioning of the Local Ministry Support Team, and the Ordination of priests. This Commissioning came after an extended period in which the Parish thought about what options it had for a sustainable future, explored ESM, and worked towards its implementation. Although the Parish was originally driven by economic necessity, their decision to implement ESM is something they have no regrets about. As Elizabeth's comments indicate, the choice in favour of ESM is something that the Parish has come to own and now feels was definitely the correct choice:

> If we hadn't, … we wouldn't be here. It's as simple as that because we didn't have any money to pay anybody. So if we hadn't chosen this way, we probably would have closed the church door and all joined another church in the town or had a home group or something like that. But because we chose this way, the Team are volunteers, they're not paid. We have our expenses paid, like petrol and any educational fees paid but we're volunteers and working as well, holding a normal job down. If we'd not done it that way financially we would not be existing. But because of the volunteer nature of the Enabler Supported Ministry there's money because everybody's still tithing and so we've actually increased our mission focus by what we're giving away and that's very exciting. (Elizabeth, teacher)

Despite problems and issues associated with some people having negative views about ESM, which were addressed, the parishioners see great benefits for the Parish through the introduction of this new way of being church, as Hester's comments indicate:

> Well, the very fact that they're still here. The church is worshipping; it makes a mark in the community; you know, it's upheld in the community as a caring church.
>
> Well it would have sort of almost bled to death financially, wouldn't it? They wouldn't have been able to support a full-time stipendiary

> priest, so they would have gone to having, probably, irregular services from a visiting priest, servicing priest, that was all. No continuity in worship, really, or sacramental worship. (Hester, retired)

The benefits experienced by the Parish through the introduction of ESM comprise a variety of activities and out-reach programmes. Among other things, these include the on-going provision of services and pastoral care at Medea Park (the local nursing home), the provision of cooking skill classes for the community, the provision of Religious Education in the local schools, and children's ministry in the wider community. These activities have markedly increased the Parish's involvement with the wider community and have created sustainable and strong inter-community links (that is, between the two 'communities': the faith community and the wider community).

The Parish now not only has a strong presence at major community events but they are expected, as the local Anglican church, to be regularly involved if not presiding at such events. Graham comments on the array of these official community events that the Parish of St Helens is increasingly involved with:

> I think there is a link between the wider community and the Parish. In some respects it's seen as the sort of the old established church so it's there for funerals and weddings and baptisms, but we're also called on by the fishing fleet for instance for the Blessing of the Fleet and … for Anzac Day and Remembrance Day and now, just recently, Vietnam Vets Day and VP Day, 15th of August, so that's been an increasing role. The funeral ministry seems to have a positive spread into the community. We're aware that a lot more funerals are being done just by the funeral directors themselves but we are still called for the church to be there but to be used in a positive way. (Graham, business proprietor)

In addition, the Parish is also involved with inter-church activities in the district as well as more informal community events, as Martha explains:

> Well, the church joins with other churches for Palm Sunday, the Blessing of the Fleet…. We have, in the past, when they've had a sort of a festival on the foreshore here, the Church has had a presence in the form of activities for children or one year they just had show bags that they gave away. It sort of stunned everybody because they were free from the local churches. So, we've taken part in things like that. (Martha, retired)

Parishioners are also involved in hospital visits and they "work in the Information Centre as volunteers [and] … the two Op Shops within the town" (Martha, retired). Community groups and fund-raising activities are further examples of the involvement and commitment of the parishioners of the St Helens Parish to their wider community:

> We make ourselves available to everything that happens in this community as a one-on-one or as a Team. We get involved in everything that goes on, everything community wise. Or we do things like have functions to get the community to come to us and get involved. Our craft group is a community get together. (Barbara, retired)

> We can probably meet more demands that are asked of us but there are so many that you could never, ever meet them all…. But, it does enable you to meet more and I think the … monthly luncheon and a decision to always give that money away has enabled us to meet more requests. There are 11 a year; 11 organizations or requests that are met through those luncheons and ... they were originally started just for some fellowship amongst ourselves but they have grown to be a community event. (Melanie, retired)

Karen comments on the on-going provision of services and pastoral care at Medea Park by the Parish, which has become increasingly shouldered by the Anglicans alone:

> Medea Park is the elderly citizens home and we take a service there, supposedly shared ministry with the Uniting Church but due to their circumstances of lack of people and lack of a permanent Minister, it seems to be falling more and more to the Anglican Church. So I would possibly take three services out of four each month. (Karen, retired)

Another example of a creative Parish response to community needs is the planned provision of cooking skills classes for the community by the Parish, as Melanie explains:

> Well, they think they'd like to run a cooking group for men who've been left on their own and really have no expertise in the kitchen. And to try to reach, too, some of the younger parents who find it very difficult to balance the budget; to help them with nutritious cheap

> meals and to try and replace a lot of the junk food in their diet. To me, I think it's an uphill battle but we can try. (Melanie, retired)

The provision of children's ministry by the Parish, while clearly religious in nature (even Anglican), is nevertheless well-received by the local community in St Helen's. Such ministry includes an annual fun day, religious education in the local schools, and a regular children's group, as Karen discusses:

> Well, before the Sunday school begins each year they have a big sort of what would equate to the old fashioned Sunday school picnic. They have a Fun Day which is totally free for all children of the community. Though it is a lead in to Sunday School starting and that's very well received both by the children of the Parish and any visitors that might happen to be around on that particular day. It's now been going for, I think, about three or four years and it's very well received.
>
> Well, there is the religious education in school. It varies year to year, depending on the principal and the manpower available from Grades 3 to 6. So some of last year's Grade 6 had wanted to continue with Scripture this year and I believe they were making a deputation to the Principal. I don't know what happened there but they wanted it to continue and I'm sure that Elizabeth will do all she can to meet that need. St Marys has JAM as it's called, Jesus and Me, for the children. The only children's activity in the whole town, Christian or non-Christian. That is very well received, too. It has a waiting list of children to attend. (Karen, retired)

In each instance, these stronger links with the community reflect the degree to which the introduction of ESM to the Parish of St Helens has allowed the Parish to look outward in care of the community rather than simply be concerned with inward-looking issues of raising a stipend for the stipendiary priest. It may seem repetitive to keep making this point, but the fact is that parishes following the stipendiary model of ministry and lacking adequate funds to pay the stipend are inevitably going to be focussed on money. This salient fact underlines the extraordinary value arising from a form of church that embraces social and cultural context and change, rather than resisting social and cultural context and change.

Changes Within the Parish as a Result of the Introduction of Enabler Supported Ministry

The introduction of Enabler Supported Ministry within the Parish of St Helens (Break O'Day) has seen the Parish move from a state of constant uncertainty and anxiety about the future to a period of stability the likes of which have not been experienced by the Parish for a couple of decades. That the Parish has now been Commissioned as an ESM parish for almost a decade is an indicator of this stability and, in turn, this stability has led to the Parish being able to engage with the wider community. The number of changes and the on-going nature of the uncertainty caused by these changes prior to the introduction of ESM to the Parish is evident in the following comments made by one parishioner:

> Well 20 years ago we had … Cedric Thomas and he'd been here for … quite a number of years. He retired and went to Sydney. After him came Ian Marshall and I don't know how many years he was here for but when we came here back in '84, John de Groote was the Rector…. It was during John de Groote's time that the organist became an ordained priest which was Kelvin Viney. So the Parish at that stage had two ordained priests and one lay reader…. After John de Groote left I think we had a gap, quite a long gap. We were under the oversee of Fingal there for a while…. And then Warwick Humphries came. We didn't realise at the time how sick Warwick Humphries was and he had two long periods while he was Rector here on sick leave which made the Parish then, because of the training and the teaching and handover from John, realise that we had to get in and do it ourselves. I suppose that was sort of the beginning of, in a way, of Enabler Supported Ministry, way back then. It wasn't called anything then.
>
> After Warwick resigned because of ill health, then Roger Hesketh came. Roger had built on the situation that had been happening when there were people who had been operating on their gifts and he built on those gifts encouraging people… [and] by that stage there were another two lay readers or three lay readers appointed so it was quite a team of people. (Tom, retired)

As with Channel/Cygnet the gifts of the laity had already been exercised and encouraged, particularly by their last Rector. Thus, despite the change and unsettled state of the Parish for many years, the experience of lay ministry afforded a good foundation on which ESM was able to develop and build, as Tom comments:

> But as far as Enabler Supported Ministry goes, well, I believe that even way back then the Lord was raising up those people because their gifts were certainly coming out in the congregation. People could see it and consequently those people who made up the Ministry Team were already undertaking some form of leadership in those particular areas. Now, it was suggested to us that we might like to go down this path by the Diocese and then, for the next, I think about 18 months, we explored that ... with many meetings and then the Parish actually took a vote at an Annual Meeting. That vote was unanimous that we go down the path of Enabler Supported Ministry. (Tom, retired)

Compared to some of the other parishes examined, St Helens was fortunate in its recent history in that the Parish had been forced to rely on its lay readers and had priests over the years that had supported a strong development of lay participation and leadership in services for the Parish. The Parish, rather than having to rely on locums or supply priests or the occasional visit from a visiting priest, now have the capacity, as Tom's quote indicates, to provide regular sacramental ministry from within the local context, thus ensuring that the parishioners are able to participate fully in receiving the sacraments:

> Well, in this situation at the present moment, there are two of the Local Ministry Support Team that are Locally Ordained. That means the Bishop has licensed them to carry out the necessary sacramental ministry that is reserved for the ordained person, which then makes the Parish just the same as any other parish. There is someone, or some people, in this situation that can carry out those sacramental roles that are normally reserved for the priest. (Tom, retired)

There are two services at St Helens on a Sunday morning as well as one at St Marys and another at Pyengana. The service times at St Helens are at 8.00 a.m. and 10.30 a.m. in the morning. The earlier service is a traditional Anglican Communion Service (Eucharist) with hymns and following an order of service from the Prayer Book (*A Prayer Book for Australia*). Parishioners have responded very positively to having this sacramental worship available to them on a regular basis, as can be seen from the following comments:

> Much more life and enthusiasm within the Parish members. Everyone is happy with whatever service they go to. I mean our 8 o'clock service; we're getting up to 25 now. And I think the fellowship after church, just having a coffee. In fact it was only last Sunday someone said to me, isn't this a great idea? You know, it's just such a lovely fellowship time. (Karen, retired)

The later service uses an outline of the order of service from the Prayer Book but often includes participation with children and is less formal than the earlier service. However, the earlier service remains the largest service in terms of attendance. Those who attend either service meet between the services for morning tea (as well as sharing in the wider life of the Parish, too). And, as Martha comments, there is good will between both congregations.

> Well, I think the change in the type of service; like the 10:30 now, we don't have the prayer book so much. We don't have a hymn book. We have more like songs and choruses. I'd rather have a few more hymns but then I suppose I'm getting up towards the older people who always don't like change. But yes, I think the changing of our 10:30 service to a more modern service or user friendly service with the overhead projector and I hated that at first. When I saw it in the church I just wanted to back out and go home but I've come to get used to it. So I suppose we can get used to all things if they're introduced properly and with explanation. One of my hopes for the church ... this might sound as though I'm being a bit frivolous is the see the pews go and individual seating in the church. For two reasons; one, the number of people in our congregation with back problems and frail elderly people who need the support of arms of a chair to stand, and also then the church can be used for other things. That's something where attitudes would have to be changed. The church is a church and not used for anything else but, in time, I think that could be changed. (Martha, retired)

Prior to the introduction of ESM, over a period from fifteen to twenty years ago, there was a constantly dwindling number of people attending church services, along with a decline in financial well-being. The Parish, as Tom's comments indicate, now has a large group attending worship services as well as participating in the wider life of the Parish and community:

> You know, you've got to have a certain number to make a parish viable. With St Marys there; I can remember going up there for years for three people. That has now grown to roughly, approximately, 11 or 12 each week. And they are solid Christian people. They're not just there because it's the done thing to do, to go to church. The same here at St Helens.
>
> Now, I believe what we've got in our congregations are solid Christians. Certainly, I know for a fact there's been nothing mentioned about tithing or money in the Parish for probably somewhere in the vicinity of eight, nine years. But yet, our getting each week is up round the $500 to $600 mark as an average. It's nothing to bank $2,000 or $3,000 of a Monday. And people just seem committed to the work of God, more so than what they have been in the past. (Tom, retired)

The increase in the numbers of those attending worship services as well as participating in the wider life of the Parish and community has brought about both a period of stability within the Parish as well a sense of optimism about the future and the role of the Parish within the wider community. In addition, without the pressure on finding the funds to pay for a stipendiary priest there is a greater care being shown by the parishioners for each other and a sharing of responsibility for the life of the Parish. There is also an increase in the subsequent sense of 'ownership' of the future of the Parish, as Melanie's observations indicate:

> Well, as I already said, the responsibilities are shared. And I think, too, now we have this evening where we've prepared goals for the future and actually put down in black and white all the things that we do and would like to do. I don't think there was anything that we do that we would like to get rid of. We can see where we're going and what we're aiming for and I'm sure this should be a benefit to all parishioners. To myself, I feel that it is. It's just nice to see it on paper and to see what we're aiming at. (Melanie, retired)

The support across the Parish, and the 'ownership' of the future of the Parish, has seen a greater participation from all members of the Parish in the life of the Parish and in the wider community as they share in the workload. The following comments from Barbara and Hester indicate that there is a real sense of people working together for the common good:

> They've helped with readings in church, assisting us with other things that need doing like in pastoral care and I only have to ring up and someone is there to help me. Generally, it's just sharing the load of the things that those people who are away would normally do. We get a lot of support from the other parishioners.
>
> I think it's made the people stronger. The Team willingly accepts the running of the Parish and support each other with that. It spreads the workload. Whereas one priest did it, we at least have five Team members who are doing the workload with the help of other parishioners. There are more of us and we are spread out in the community and we make sure we are out in the community. (Barbara, retired)
>
> I don't think that the Ministry Team could operate and grow and be sustainable without the loving prayerful support of the community here in this Parish. And I feel they've got that, totally. (Hester, retired)

This sense of people working together for the common good does not mean that difficult issues are avoided, or that there is a false sense of 'niceness' that does not allow for serious discussions to take place about the future of the Parish. One of the inclusive elements that would have been rejected before the introduction of ESM within the Parish is the participation of women in the full life of the Parish, including sacramental and pastoral ministry. Previously women were restricted to stereotypical roles within the Parish (that is, cooking, cleaning, etc.) but now, as the following comments from Melanie and Tom indicate, women expect to, and do, participate fully in the life of the Parish and this is accepted:

> [W]e have a woman now who is a lay reader and we have had a woman lay reader in the past who wasn't well received to start with … from the point of view that the people didn't like taking communion from a woman. But I think we've gone beyond that because we have a female Eucharistic assistant. And then, of course, we have Barbara who does a lot of the duties of a lay reader and a lot of visiting and I don't think it would bother most people now. (Melanie, retired)
>
> I think the women play just as an important role. There's certainly a lot of consultation amongst the Team. Not so much at meetings but certainly over the telephone and after Church, over a cuppa and those sort of things. And not just with the Team but with the whole Parish.

> Yes, so I think everyone is very important, whether they be male or female. (Tom, retired)

There is also a recognition of what could be loosely categorized as the twin effects of contemporary society on women and the church; namely, that women are now seen as having the capacity to be ordained while at the same time the changing role of women has resulted in the cessation of church groups that women formerly belonged to. Commenting on these issues, Martha observes that she

> can see … two … ladies who could very well be ordained. Whether they would be, I don't know but, in my eyes, they have the abilities to be ordained. And the changing role in society of women has impacted greatly on our church in that I see that as one of the reasons for the Guild having to fold because young mothers and even women with their children who have left school, are back in the work force and they just don't have the time. (Martha, retired)

One of the female members of the Local Ministry Support Team has now been Ordained as a Priest (on 4/11/06) and exercises full pastoral and sacramental life within the Parish. This would have been unthinkable in this Parish only a decade ago.

There has been an increase in the Pastoral Offices (baptisms, weddings and funerals) taken within the Parish compared to fifteen to twenty years ago. This, in turn, as Melanie's comments indicate, has made the Parish feel that it has regained the respect of the wider community and is not seen as being irrelevant any longer by those who do not attend church:

> Well, according to the marriage register I think the number of weddings, and I'm not sure but I think baptisms as well, seems to have risen and in today's society I think that's encouraging that people are still seeking out the church for a Christian marriage. (Melanie, retired)

Although St Helen's has a large increase in population during the holiday season it has also experienced a permanent growth in population over recent years. Part of the increased association with the church, including increased attendance, may be due, as Barbara suggests, to the advent of so many new people moving into the district:

> In this sort of holiday place we do get a floating population and it changes quite a bit. We have a very stable base in the Anglican Church here made up of people who have come into the town from all walks of life.... I think the stable base is growing with more people retiring. (Barbara, retired)

The introduction of Enabler Supported Ministry within the Parish of St Helens (Break O' Day) has led to a renewed self-confidence. The Parish is now able to sustain its sacramental and pastoral life and to engage in the life of the wider community. Despite the difficulties that surrounded the introduction of Enabler Supported Ministry within the Parish there is now, as Tom's comments indicate, an acceptance of Enabler Supported Ministry, even from those who objected to it when it was first proposed:

> I think now, if you ask them, I'd be surprised if anyone wanted to go back to the old way of having a rector ... I've heard a couple of older people talking about Enabler Supported Ministry that were probably very much against it to start with and they've been asked questions about it and their replies have been very much for it. (Tom, retired)

Further to this, as Tom observes, those most actively involved in the life of the Parish feel supported in their roles and they feel that they are valued and that they have the friendship of those from the Parish as a whole:

> I find I get on very well with people. Not as a priest but as a friend but I'm welcome as a priest in those situations. (Tom, retired)

And, finally, the following quote from Hester indicates how the Parish is looking forward to remaining 'alive and well' and continuing to participate in, and engage with, the life of the wider community:

> I think it's tremendous. I think it's alive and well. I think sometimes they sell themselves short but that's the benefit of coming in and seeing it working from an outside point of view. (Hester, retired)

St Helens – Further Changes in the Parish and Municipality

St Helens and the surrounding districts have seen remarkable and consistent change over the last decade or so. In the last few years, such change has escalated. The Parish of St. Helens has adapted to such change, and, indeed has embraced change as they have responded to the needs of those in the wider community in the continually changing municipality in which they are situated.

1. New Educational Opportunities

Since having become an ESM parish, St Helens has experienced on-going change – people come and go, children grow up and leave, older people die or move away. In summary, the community demographics have changed and keep changing and keep changing again. For example, St Helens had the image of being solely a retirement town or a holiday town. This is not the case any more. Enrolments are increasing at the local school and businesses are expanding. Building costs are at a premium and there is a wait of least 18 months to get any building work done. The rapidity of change is astounding. There are more and more cars around the town, and parking is now at a premium, a situation that arose after the introduction of the new ferries across Bass Strait.

The increase in the permanent population has increased the need for educational training in the town. The provision of education used to be only available to Year 10. This meant, as Elizabeth explains, that young people who wanted to pursue their education left the area and never returned:

> [T]he school only went to Year 10 and so if you wanted to go on to university or TAFE it meant leaving ... The other thing that happened in the community was with those children leaving [means] that age group is out of the community and most of them never come back. Once they see what the cities offer and they go to university then their jobs take them wherever, well anywhere in the world really. I don't know what the stats would be on that [young people returning] but it would be very low. (Elizabeth, teacher)

To address this problem the North East Education and Training Centre (NEET) opened in 1999 with 8 students. NEET now enrols around 20 students. This facility accommodates students in Years 11 and 12, providing them with the opportunity to pursue an education in St Helens instead of traveling to Hobart or Launceston. This makes it easier for families and young people in that it means that "15 and 16 year olds are not having to leave home, go to the big city and cope with all that as well as with their studies" (Melanie, retired). The result is that St Helens now has many students in the 15-20 year-old age group in town all week, and not just at the weekends.

However, the provision of courses by NEET, while enhancing educational opportunities for young people in the St Helens area, is limited, as Elizabeth explains:

> Their courses that they're offering are limited so depending what your vocation needs are will depend whether you stay or not. That has changed the demographics of the town in that that group 15 to 20 are now about town. (Elizabeth, teacher)

Further, the change in demographics of the area has also encouraged local businesses to offer traineeships and work opportunities for this mid-teen age-group:

> And just in recent months Chickenfeed and Dougherty's have opened here and that has provided work for the younger people as well as traineeships. (Melanie, retired)

In addition, there has been a noticeable change in the overall numbers in the school system, as can be seen from Elizabeth's comments:

> The school population has changed in that three years ago they had their biggest intake of kinder for a long, long time. So the school population has changed, the teachers have increased, so there's been quite an impact which means that the age of the town must be lowering. It's not now seen as a retirement town. I don't know what the mean age is at the moment but certainly it has to have dropped. So there are young families here now as well. (Elizabeth, teacher)

Responding to changed demographics, with St Helens now seen as a desirable place to live as well as a retirement destination, educational opportunities have increased and expanded and the Parish, also responding to this changed demographic, has changed and expanded the services it offers to be inclusive of young families and their needs.

2. The Impact of the Tree-Changers and Sea-Changers

The Anglican welfare agency, Anglicare, have been working in St Helens for a number of years. In 2002, the Parish provided accommodation for Anglicare in the recently re-furbished Parish centre. The Parish also distributes furniture, blankets and other household items as well as food to those in need, as the Anglicare budget is inadequate to meet such demands.

This work with Anglicare clearly demonstrates the nature of some of the changes that have happened in the Parish and municipality. When Rev Collins first began working at St Helens in September, 2001, the town was run-down and there was a real sense of loss within the region: loss of a way of life where everyone knew everyone else, loss of the fishing industry, a steadily declining population, and no real hope for the future. St Marys was in an even more run-down state and real estate in the town could not be sold as no one wanted to move into the area (other than squatters who moved into vacant houses when someone died and no family wanted to live in the house). However, as Elizabeth's comments indicate, despite the high unemployment rate and the sense of loss there was a degree of affordability about the region and low income earners were able to live in the region and raise families in relative comfort; fishing supplemented many diets, and the 'laid-back' beach lifestyle had its own attractions:

> Very laid back. I remember when we moved the children were still in high school and I went to my very first parents and friends meeting and I dressed as I did for Scottsdale which was a skirt and jumper and high heels. Walked in and I was totally over dressed, like, where am I? Everybody was casual; shorts, t-shirts. So there's this seaside laid back... in fact, we were told when we were moving, when you get there don't go "coasty", which is a term meaning laid-back, surf all day, work when you run out of money, if you don't feel like going today, don't go. And that attitude was everywhere. (Elizabeth, teacher)

Over the past five years, though, real estate prices have continued to increase steadily as retirees from elsewhere move into the region. This has resulted in many of those who were low income earners or on social security support being forced out of St Helens because they could no longer afford to live there. Initially, such people moved to St Marys; but then as real estate became more sought after in St Marys many of those who were on fixed or low incomes were forced out further along the Fingal Valley to Avoca, Mathinna, Rossarden, or Fingal. In effect, these towns have become poverty traps and there are many social problems in them. Alongside Anglicare, the Parish of St Helens specifically helps these people who have been disadvantaged by demographic changes in the area:

> The increase in property prices has meant that private rental markets have risen … because the property is more valuable. They have to pay more in rent and of course pensions don't rise with the property values so there's been a shortfall there. There's a lot of single parent families and I think they just find it a plain struggle to meet the demands that there are on their pensions and they turn to Anglicare to fill the gap somewhat. (Martha, retired)

This process of rising property prices pushing those on low incomes or social security out of St Helens and then St Marys replicates a similar situation in the south of the State. People who lived in either Brighton or Bridgewater have similarly been forced to move first to New Norfolk and then to the upper Derwent Valley to such towns as Maydena and Westerway. These towns exhibit similar social problems and dysfunction to those in the north-east of the State.

Therefore, the arrival of the 'sea-changers' and 'tree-changers' to St Helens and St Marys, respectively, has not been without tangible negative consequences to many in the area. The Parish has sought to address this situation by provision of food relief and furniture (see below for further discussion) to those who are adversely affected by increasing real estate prices.

3. From Looking In to Looking Out

In addressing the problems and issues created by the influx of newcomers into the area, one of the responses by the Parish of St Helens is what they call a 'furniture ministry'. Through their association with the work of Anglicare, the Parish had first hand experience of the plight of some members of the wider community, as Elizabeth explains:

> With Anglicare comes a group of people who are needing support and we've found that the two needs have been equipping them with things for their home and food. So we now have a container at the back of the church where people bring food every Sunday and that's distributed at the Anglicare counsellor's discretion. The furniture is through the point of contact with him. So he arranges a rented property, or they find their own rented property, and then they need things. And people in the community are giving up furniture, instead of it going to the tip it comes to us. Some still goes to the tip because it's not suitable. So we've now developed a system where we've got furniture stored and it's just turning over all the time. (Elizabeth, teacher)

The 'furniture ministry' is a rather ingenious 'distribution' plan that connects two apparently unrelated results of the demographic changes experienced in the St Helens area in recent years. It is, in a way, a variation of the 'Robin Hood' theme, where the wealth of the well-off (their donations) is given to the poor.

Those retiring to St Helens, and the 'tree changers' and 'sea-changers', often do not settle permanently. There is a variety of reasons that people do not stay: ranging from the need for easy access to large hospitals in the cities (this is often the reason retirees move on) to relocation to the 'mainland' to the increasingly apparent phenomenon of the 'grey nomad'. This is a remarkable and new phenomenon characterizing retirees in recent years. There is also a sort of 'slow-motion grey nomadism', where retirees settle for a while and become part of the community, but then move after a few years and repeat the process elsewhere. Such people are often in a position to donate large quantities of good quality furniture to the Parish. Sometimes there are whole households of furniture and household items.

At the same time, there are people who are financially destitute or struggling on low incomes or benefits. These people have been pushed further and further out, because they cannot afford the increasing rents, into areas where there are no work opportunities. These people are in need of the provision of furniture because they have no funds to purchase such items. The Parish redistributes the donations of furniture from the 'haves' who donate the furniture to the 'have-nots' who need the furniture, as can be seen in Karen's comments:

> The furniture that is being donated is picked up and stored in one of two places, a garage or a very large shed that we have, and people come to Tom with their needs. He knows what's in the furniture shed and he can just say, yes or no, we have a fridge, we have a washing machine, we have beds. Beds seem to be the biggest thing, the majority of things that are donated and also the majority of things that are asked for.
>
> So the things come in, they're in the shed for a while, there's a need and they go out of the shed. (Karen, retired)

Such is the need for this 'furniture ministry' that it is quite extensive, but it is carried out by parishioners who volunteer their time. This ministry is so well known about in the community that people leaving the area will often just drop off items, knowing they will be put to good use. An interesting feature of the ministry is that items often have a cyclical existence:

> We're given it so we give it away and it just keeps turning over. Sometimes if people leave town they'll give it back and you'll get

> the same things back. So it's just a complete circle. It's amazing. (Elizabeth, teacher)
>
> Often if people go to leave the area they will donate them back. Just seems to be a continuous cycle of donation and giving out. (Karen, retired)

The furniture that is donated and distributed where needed is of good quality. No furniture is given away if it is unfit for use (the measure being: "would you use this?"). The Parish has a free Tip Pass and any unusable furniture is disposed of at the local tip. Moreover, the Parish of St Helens makes no money from this ministry. While the donated items could be sold in an Op Shop, an option that is often used by parishes as a fund-raising venture to keep struggling parishes viable, the Parish has decided to donate rather than to sell on. This is because of the cultural framework undergirding ESM that encourages enrichment of the wider community through an outward-focused expression of their Christian faith.

Nor does the Parish exploit any person's vulnerability by using this as an exercise to proselytize: the furniture is given as a gift of love and care with no expectation that anyone to whom the furniture is given should come to church:

> The Parish doesn't charge anything at all. Whatever the need is, if we can meet it from our storeroom the people are given it. But they are told it is a gift from the Anglican Church. That's the only sort of thing. They don't get preached at or anything like that. They're just told it's a gift from the Anglican Church and it's left at that. (Karen, retired)

The 'furniture ministry' is an excellent example of the outward looking mission of the church. It is both 'missional' and 'not missional'. It is 'missional' (because it is theologically grounded) in the sense of being undertaken as a way of living out their faith. Yet, it is 'not missional' (because 'missional' is often described as proselytizing) in the sense that it is a social-justice exercise to help the needy that is done without any expectation of getting people to come to church. In addition, many of the people helped actually live in towns outside the Break O'Day Municipality and Parish. These are often towns that are located in the Northern Midlands Municipality and Parish. Thus, the parishioners of St Helens are extending help and assistance to people who are not even a part of their own wider community. There is an 'elective affinity' between the beliefs of this group and their social context.

This is facilitated by the model of church ministry that is ESM, where there is an embracing of social and cultural context through the cultural beliefs and actions of the faith community.

4. From Stability to Constant Change

The existence of the 'furniture ministry' attests to two trends in the St Helens area and represents the most visible sign of change within both the Parish and region. Firstly, there is a cycle of renewal within St Helens, which has seen an increase in population and the outward prosperity of the town and region, along with a hidden poverty, which has been 'sanitized' in the public sphere by those affected being forced out of the town and the region. Secondly, there is an increasing mobility that has seen the town and region move from a very stable community to one that is now in a constant state of flux and change.

Despite the recent influx of younger people moving to the town and district there are still many older residents. This seems to be a similar phenomenon across Tasmania (particularly within the Anglican Church). A repeated lament across almost all parishes is: "where are the children and the youth?" However, Tasmania is attracting people moving into the State who are older and can retire here on their superannuation or other income. This is causing a gradual increase in an aging population compounded by the fact that many in the under 45 year-old population are often forced to leave the State to seek either work or educational opportunities. That is, a significant component in the growth in the State's population is from migration not just from natural increase.

This demographic phenomenon is not understood by those who grew up in the 'builder' or the 'boomer' generations who expect to see children and youth in the same proportions to the overall population that they experienced in their childhood and youth. This demographic phenomenon is coupled to a number of contemporary social processes which have seen the subtle movement in patterns of religion from 'obligation to consumption' (Davie 2006) and to the change in outlook between the modern and the post-modern (Lyon 2002). As the following quote from Tom indicates these trends are just as evident in St Helens as they are around the entire State:

> Well, 20 years ago it was very much a sleepy little fishing village. And there were people who used to holiday here who had been holidaying here for 30 and 40 years, every Christmas. It was certainly controlled

> by the old names or the old families in those days and they didn't go much on change. They wanted things to just remain as they were. Well, in the last 3 or 4 years there has been dramatic change in the town with retirees moving here from the mainland, mainly from NSW and Victoria but quite a few from WA. So they've seen an upmarket in property values and an upmarket in the number of shops in the town and businesses and also in the numbers at school and everywhere else in the town. So we've had that influx. (Tom, retired)

While increases in population do not automatically mean increased numbers attending church, the Parish of St Helens has nevertheless experienced a steady growth, and this is despite continually losing people though illness, death or migration. Many of those who choose to move to the St Helens area are in a financial position to support the church and have the time and energy to give to working for the church, and any other community group that they choose. Melanie gives a lovely example of this 'help' the Parish has experienced from newcomers to the area:

> Well, I think numbers are slowly, slowly improving. We've lost quite a lot of parishioners through moving away and through death and some of them just drift off. But we have had replacements and some of them have been well almost miraculous. Like when we were an organist short, Graham came out one morning and said who's going to play for us today? And nobody did. We stood up and we sang the first hymn without accompaniment. We got to the second hymn, someone walked down the aisle and sat down at the piano and you could tell they were very used to playing and he has been playing at the 8 o'clock service, I don't know, it must be two, three, four years since then… I'm sure it was a tongue in cheek comment from Graham to start with and there was someone in the congregation with that skill. Yes, there have been other instances where people have come and had a gift that we've needed. (Melanie, retired)

As mentioned before, though, one of the main reasons that people leave the town and the region is because of inadequate health services and facilities. This can cause enormous emotional and financial stress on many who are too unwell to make such a change or who do not have the financial resources to move back to the 'mainland' or to Hobart or Launceston. This adds a significant burden to the already over-taxed health professionals and services and facilities in the town and the region and is, in a large measure, one of the reasons why rural regions in Tasmania have such difficulty attracting permanent health professionals to them.

St Helens was once a fishing town or just a retirement town for retired farmers from the North-West of the State, who had their holiday shacks in St Helens and took their holidays in the town each year. Now the town and district have been transformed, and nearby Binalong Bay is considered a highly desirable and luxurious holiday destination. Whereas previously it consisted of a few shacks and very few permanent residents, it now attracts large numbers of tourists each year as well as an increasing number of permanent residents. However, this change comes at a cost; the greatest cost being borne by the poorest sector of the community.

However, there is also the emotional 'cost' to those who feel that St Helens and the region have lost something that they look back on as being the defining characteristic of the town and the region. Even the small township of Pyengana has changed: the 'Pub in the Paddock' and the cheese factory are clear indicators that the former way of life in the dairy industry in this 'green hollow' now requires entrepreneurial skill and a capacity to be creative and imaginative so as to engage with the future. As Hester and Tom's comments indicate, change has become a constant part of the life of the Parish and of the wider community:

> I think they've seen the need for change and they've reacted in a very positive way. (Hester, retired)

> So much change goes on here. There's been a terrific amount of change even in the town of St Helens. When Anglicare first came here and we were working with the furniture, we were delivering furniture here in St Helens. That was the only place we seemed to deliver it. With the increase of property values all of a sudden we found ourselves not delivering in St Helens so much but heading up to St Marys. There wasn't a Sunday go past that either Graham or I were taking a load of furniture to deliver after the service. Just recently we have been actually not delivering it to St Marys so much but heading to Fingal, which is the next town down the Fingal Valley, because that's where the people are moving to because of the low rent. So it's changing. Even the community is changing so

> dramatically and that's been in the last sort of three years. So we've noticed that in three years. (Tom, retired)

Thus, in the midst of change, it seems that those parishes that can engage with change and become vital parts of their communities are more than likely to have a sustainable future. St Helens Parish is an example, because of the way of being church that ESM has fostered, of embracing social and cultural change, rather than resisting it, for the enrichment of both the church and the wider community. This process of change within the church has left some with a sense of loss (of the rector and the power and status which the Anglican church enjoyed formerly within Tasmanian society); however, as the following quotes indicate, many are finding this to be quite a liberating time and are looking forward to the future with hope:

> I don't know in what form. It may … [change] again but it's weathered the big change and they've shown they can do it; that their trust is in God and they are willing to be led and they'll be all right. They'll be all right; yes. (Hester, retired)

> We've now got people who are doing things in the name of the church that they would never had done if we'd had a rector. A lot by their own initiative and a lot by "You can do it", giving permission to do it. So, for instance, the case recently where one of our senior members was dying. [He] had a long involvement with the church and two couples, particularly, were the ones who ministered. The Team were informed what was happening and were called in at times but those two couples took the brunt of the whole ministry and the lead up to him dying and it was just amazing. And really just lovely to see that they actually could do it. Probably five years ago if you'd said that they were doing that they wouldn't have believed you. (Elizabeth, teacher)

Church out-reach activities such as the 'furniture ministry' and caring for their own dying parishioners may go unspoken of on the world stage, yet what this Parish has achieved through its implementation of ESM is quite extraordinary for a small group of Anglicans in a small rural Tasmanian town. Enabler Supported Ministry has encouraged an expression of their faith that would not have been thought possible a decade earlier. Hester's comments about their ministry are tinged, quite rightly, with unmistakable satisfaction in what they are doing:

> Well, at the lay ministry weekend when we were at a workshop, having to fill out, do we do this, do we do that and numbers one to ten. They were sort of round five or six and I was giving them ten for all these things. Because ... I said, "But you do that. You do it". "Oh yes, well perhaps we do". Yes, their goals are high. And yeah, I think they have to say, "We're doing okay. We're doing all right". (Hester, retired)

Conclusion

The parishioners at St Helens have moved from an inward focus to an outward focus of caring for all in their community, and in the process they have found new life for themselves, too. The outward focus that is manifest in the Parish of St Helens, and the new life that has come from such an attitude, is a story of hope about how impressive results can grow from small beginnings and about how ESM provides a way of being church that engages in the social and cultural context.

However, the story of St Helens, and the other parishes, also functions as a critique of the 'success' oriented programme-type agenda of the 'purpose driven church' focussed on increasing the numbers of people attending church and the amount of money they give. This type of church-growth model has been marketed in Tasmania at various conferences over the years extolling the virtues of this style of church and also at such evangelistic crusades as the Franklin Graham 'Festival Tasmania' in 2005. These types of crusades and conferences promote a model of church that pays no heed to the social or cultural context. The post-modern world is characterized by fluidity and pluralism that guarantees change and unpredictability. To be healthy, churches need to acknowledge and work with such plurality and fluidity, not against it. Churches do not exist outside society and culture, and the ethnographic study of these four rural Anglican communities of faith allows us to not only tell their stories and share them but also to interpret these stories.

In so doing, ESM as a new model of church ministry is shown to be one example of a synergy between belief and social and cultural context. The underlying Weberian orientation in this book points to the relationship between belief and action being a crucial factor of why ESM has enabled this Parish (and the other three parishes) to flourish. As such, it illuminates a possible direction by which church congregations can 'be church' and 'be more than church' and thereby allow an engagement with and an enrichment of their wider communities. These parishioners have learnt that the "sign of a true vocation is not a miracle, but service for the benefit of the community" (Küng 1983: 486). The story of St Helens is a story of service, as seen in their 'furniture ministry' to those in need in the wider community.

The community of faith at St Helens is totally immersed in the life of the wider community and the wider community see the Parish as being relevant to their lived experience. The change to ESM has facilitated a change in culture to the community of faith and this change has, in turn, resulted in a change in the social organization of the Parish that has brought about a sustainable, outward-looking and engaged community of faith. And as Hester says of the St Helens Parish and their connection to and service of the wider community, "We're doing all right". Compared to how the Parish was before the introduction of ESM this is surely something of an understatement.

A Chronology of Events

1998: the Diocese appoints a priest (Claude) as the Diocesan Ministry Officer (1998-2002).

October 1999: the Parish Council voted unanimously to pursue this new way of being church.

November 1999: the Parish began a 5-week 'Journey of Discovery' for developing this so called Collaborative Ministry. At the end of this 5-week 'Journey of Discovery' the Parish decided to continue exploring this new way of being church and appointed a steering committee. An Enabler's role was outlined, along with a commitment to embark on an education programme in February 2000.

March 2000: another education programme commenced after the Ash Wednesday Service on the 8th of March exploring the nature of Local Collaborative Ministry (LCM/ESM).

June 2000: the Parish farewelled the then (and last) Rector.

July 2000: another workshop on LCM (ESM) was held.

August 2000: the Annual General Meeting was held where a unanimous decision was made in favour of the Parish becoming a LCM (ESM) parish.

October 2000: was set aside as a month of prayer and reflection, with the Calling Out process set for the 29th of October. The Parish Council agreed on the following areas of ministry to which parishioners would be called: teaching, administration, children's ministry, pastoral care, evangelism, prayer and healing as well as Locally Ordained Priests. A Local Ministry Support Team was formed and began to meet fortnightly.

Team members were 'Called Out' to specific ministries: Co-ordinator of Pastoral Care – Barbara Hand; Co-ordinator of Administration – Michael Wakefield; Co-ordinator of Teaching – Alexander Withers; Co-ordinator of Evangelism, Prayer and Healing – Alexander & Carole Withers; Co-ordinator of Children's Ministry – Wendy Holland; Locally Ordained Ministry – Michael Wakefield and Alexander Withers

13th of December 2000: the Parish held a special service to mark the beginning of the Formation Stage of Development of LCM.

July 2001: Diocesan visitation to Parish to determine whether the Parish was ready to be Commissioned.

August 2001: Ordination candidates interviewed by the Bishop. Ordination to the Diaconate of 10 people Called to Ordained ministry from five parishes (Channel/Cygnet, New Norfolk, St Helens, Circular Head, Sheffield) on 30/8/01.

1st September 2001: James Collins begins as Enabler to parishes of Channel/Cygnet, New Norfolk and St Helens.

3rd October 2001: James Collins Commissioned as Enabler to parishes of Channel/Cygnet, New Norfolk and St Helens.

13th February 2002: On Ash Wednesday, the 13th of February, 2002, the Portland Memorial Hall in St Helens was packed with some 250 local people to witness and participate in the service to mark the official launch of Enabler Supported Ministry in the Parish of St Helens, including the Commissioning of parishioners, the Commissioning of the Local Ministry Support Team (Barbara Hand, Wendy Holland Michael Wakefield, Carole Withers and Alexander Withers) and the Ordination of priests (Michael Wakefield and Alexander Withers).

May 2002: The Diocesan Ministry Officer (Claude) leaves the Diocese.

28th February 2007: James Collins resigns as Enabler to the Parish of St Helens.

Chapter Five: The Parish of Hamilton

Introduction

This chapter outlines how the changed church structure, from stipendiary priest to Enabler Supported Ministry, within the Parish of Hamilton has allowed the Parish to engage with the social and cultural context in the wider community. Because of this attitude of engagement with social and cultural change that ESM engenders, parishioners have strengthened their relationship with those in their wider community. The chapter also outlines how the role of the Enabler, which had been developed elsewhere in other ESM parishes, was implemented at Hamilton.

The Parish of Hamilton is a particularly interesting case study as this Parish (and the whole community generally) has been drastically affected by the plight of rural decline afflicting many regional areas in Australia. Further, the Parish is in an area of Tasmania that has not attracted an increase in population from new-comers settling in the area for the life-style or as a retirement destination, as has been the case in the three other parishes/ localities studied.

Background

Hamilton, and the surrounding region, is an archetypal rural district. Until the mid-1970's very little had changed in the district from the time that grants were given to settler families in the very early 1800's. Since the mid-1970's, though, there has been significant structural, cultural, and economic change that has affected the entire area leading to a massive decline in population, a loss of employment opportunities, the withdrawal of social infrastructure, and the steady and ever increasing aging of the population.

The effects of declining population and employment opportunities, the growth of unemployment, and the reduction in services are felt particularly strongly in rural Australia (Dempsey 1990). In addition, cultural changes in Western society have replaced the monopoly of the Christian 'world-view' with the freedom to choose alternative world-views (Bentley, Blombery & Hughes 1992). Together these changes have had a marked effect on rural towns and districts in Tasmania. While a strong rural farming community in terms of Tasmania's primary industry, the district and Parish of Hamilton, as a whole, have had to contend with serious issues and problems arising from demographic and cultural/social change.

The Central Highlands – A Description

The Central Highlands Municipality covers 8,010 square kilometres (11.6% of the state). It is the second largest Council area in the state, but has the second smallest population. The Central Highlands makes a significant and increasing contribution to the economic wealth of Tasmania through forestry, farming, power production, trout fishing, tourism, and recreation.

In the 2006 Census (Australian Bureau of Statistics 2006) the population of the Central Highlands was 2,242, decreasing 4.5% since 2001. The number of people 65 years and over was 325 or 14.5% of the total population, an increase of 14% since 2001, and 31% were persons aged 55 years and over. The median age for the Central Highlands was 43 years (compared to 37 years for people in Australia), an increase from 39 years in 2001. Projections from 2006 to 2018 predict a decrease in population by 7%. Within that total, the 75 years and over cohort is projected to increase by 100%, to stand at 9.3% of the population by 2018.

The Socio Economic Indexes for Areas (SEIFA) (Australian Bureau of Statistics 2001) indicate aspects of disadvantage that relate to income and wealth, living conditions, education, and engagement in skilled occupations. According to the SEIFA indexes, where lower numbers indicate areas of greater relative socio-economic disadvantage, the Central Highlands population is more disadvantaged compared to Tasmanians in general, and the Hobart population in particular.

Table 1: SEIFA Indexes

Index	**Central Highlands**	**Hobart**	**Tasmania**
Relative S-E Disadvantage	935.08	1,065.79	969.74
Economic Resources	869.20	1,030.79	934.54
Education and Occupation	887.17	1,137.44	962.18

Source: (Australian Bureau of Statistics 2001)

Other data indicates that employees' wages and salaries in the Central Highlands ($30,888) are below the Tasmanian average ($36,244). During the period 2001 – 2005, the proportion of Central Highland residents registered as unemployed increased from 12.3% to 13.9%. In the March quarter of 2006 the unemployment rate for the Central Highlands was 13.9%, considerably higher than the Tasmanian rate of 6.9% (Australian Bureau of Statistics 2006).

The Central Highlands is an extensive geographical area whose primary physical features include large farms, forests, and large water areas (rivers and lakes). There are many exceptional examples of early colonial architecture, though many of these are private homes on large properties that are not accessible to the public. While boasting many beautiful places, the Central Highlands is even more isolated than Channel/Cygnet or St Helens in terms of services, infrastructure, and distance to Hobart/Launceston. It is this isolation and lack of services that probably deters the 'alternative life-stylers' and 'grey nomads' from taking up residence. Though there is a trickle of people moving into the area, the declining population rate in this area continues unabated, as does the aging of the population.

The Anglican Parish of Hamilton – A Description

The Anglican Parish of Hamilton is now largely defined within the municipality of the Central Highlands. As with so many rural parishes in Tasmania, the Hamilton Parish today is the end-result of a long history of amalgamation after amalgamation (Beavan 1988). This includes amalgamations of Hamilton, Gretna, Ellendale, and Macquarie Plains or, as it is also known, Bushy Park. These amalgamations, predictably, were always done with the intent of trying to secure sufficient funds to pay for a stipendiary priest. And, as always, this 'solution' to dwindling numbers and finances was not successful and the priest was required to service more and more centres over an increasingly larger geographical area.

Currently, the Parish has six centres. There were seven centres consisting of: Osterley, Ouse, Hamilton, Ellendale, Gretna, Macquarie Plains, and Maydena, but the Parish has recently sold the centre at Maydena due to the fact that no one ever came to church there. Other centres were formerly at Pelham and Strickland, but these were closed long ago. As with the Parishes of Southern Midlands and Northern Midlands, the Parish of Hamilton covers a vast area. It is also the largest parish in the Tasmanian Diocese in terms of the geographical area it covers. The travelling distance between centres in the Parish of Hamilton can be at least 2 hours by car.

Over a number of years the Parish had, one by one, sold all the rectories attached to their various centres in order to continue funding their stipendiary priest and pay bills. Predictably, given the combination of rural decline and other demographic and social/cultural changes, this tactic was unsuccessful in the long-term. As with the other communities of faith examined for the research, and as for many rural (and increasingly urban) parishes, dwindling numbers and insoluble financial difficulties presented serious problems to the Hamilton Parish that had to be realistically dealt with.

After considering various options, the Parish chose to pursue the possibility of ESM as a way of being church. One of the interesting insights revealed in the examination of this Parish is that it demonstrates how adaptable ESM is to context. ESM provided a means of encouraging a strengthening and growth of existing ties between the church and the community that resulted in the enrichment of both, despite massive demographic changes. There is a close relationship between all the communities of faith and the communities in which they are situated, but none so tightly linked as in Hamilton. Further, in the Parish of Hamilton can be seen the extent and depth of the rural decline that has impacted on most rural areas in Australia to a greater or lesser degree and the effect this has on the local church.

Church and Community

In the Parish of Hamilton, there is a close relationship between the church and the community/society. This probably stems from the declining population in the area over many, many decades and the history of the 'squatocracy', where in early Tasmania a few wealthy families were leaders in both the community and the Anglican Church. The 'squatocracy' was predominantly Anglican, reflecting the early colonial history of the State. The Catholic Church, in contrast, had a close relationship with the convicts and the working class.

Many of those belonging to the Parish of Hamilton have been members of the Parish all of their lives. These parishioners have not moved from the district and there are not many parishioners who have moved into the district. Current parishioners are often the descendants of the same families who were given land grants in the early period of white settlement in Tasmania (or Van Diemen's Land as it was then known). These families still have the same land holdings granted to their ancestors in the early nineteenth century, some dating back to a decade or two after white settlement in the 1810's and 1820's. Although there have been enormous changes in the Central Highlands district there is still evidence of this close relationship between the community of faith and the wider community, one that has flourished under ESM.

Life in the early to mid-twentieth century had not changed markedly from when these families took up the original grants of land. Referring to life in the area in the 1940's and 1950's, and the place of the church in the community at that time, one parishioner commented that as a child she felt

> the church was very much the centre point of *everybody's* lives in the area. A great many social activities centred round the church; baptisms, weddings, funerals, were always large gatherings. As a child I certainly didn't attend funerals. In fact, most of the women didn't attend anything beyond the service. But because there were no vehicles about, really, people made their lives within the area and it was a very happy peaceable existence. Lots of picnics, lots of walking to wherever we needed to go or riding horses wherever we needed to go and there seemed to be far less pressure. (Mary, retired)

The large grants of land, along with relatively inexpensive labour, contributed to economic stability for these families for a century and a half. As can be seen from the following comments these properties typically had several families working on the farm other that the family of the owner.

> Well we had two families working on the property with their children and then there was one wonderful old man who had had polio and actually he probably wasn't all that old when he came to us.... And in those days we weren't taxed to keep people *on* our properties after they retired. They would stay. My husband's family, there were two or three elderly people who had worked for them and they just lived in cottages on the property. They were looked after if they were sick or anything happened to them; my mother-in-law looked after those people. (Mary, retired)

Even today, many of these farms still have many houses on the property that formerly housed families of the farm workers. One property, for example, has nine such houses, although they are now all empty. However, changing economic and environmental circumstances and changing farming practices in the 1960's and 1970's saw an end to these families living on the farms on which they worked. Farm mechanization during these decades substantially reduced the need for farm workers, with the result today being that many very large farms employ extremely small numbers of casual workers, if any. This population loss affected local schools, hospitals, shops, and the church.

The loss of these families from the farming properties upon which they worked was compounded by the loss of people from the 'Hydro towns'. The damming of Tasmania's rivers began early in the twentieth century in the first instance to provide water for irrigation for the farming communities where the dams were located. Later these dams grew to massive proportions with damming projects being undertaken by the Hydro Electric Commission (HEC) to provide water to generate electricity for Tasmania. The HEC envisaged that the electricity would stimulate an economic boom fuelled by the availability of a 'cheap' power source. Several towns grew-up to accommodate the workers who built these dams. These were large towns of as many as five to six thousand people living in them, with many of the workers coming from the recently war-ravaged countries of Southern Europe seeking to find a new life in Australia.

These towns, including Wayatinah, Tarraleah, Bronte Park, Butlers Gorge, Strathgordon, and Waddamana, thrived throughout the period when the dams were being built. After the construction phase was over, however, there was no work available other than for a skeleton staff of maintenance workers at each site. Therefore, the Hydro towns all effectively died and the populations which had swelled from, in many instances nothing, in the post-World War Two years left to find work elsewhere. Mary's reminiscences hint at this presence of large numbers of people in the Hydro-towns in the post-war years and the services available:

> In Wayatinah, Tarraleah, Waddamana … we had very happy weekends, actually, going up there. Oh, goodness … they *were* large towns. They were the equivalent of ... almost of New Norfolk. And they were totally self-contained; everything was there. And it was a fascinating.... I wish, now, that I had been older and more able to enjoy the privilege of meeting people from so many different countries. I mean there was an *amazing* collection of people there and Maydena was a very large area too.
>
> These places had – there was a bush brother [that is, a clergy person] operating in the Hydro camps, permanently. There was a doctor for them. There was a bush nursing area for them. And at Maydena they had their own doctor. And we had clergymen. (Mary, retired)

For the Parish of Hamilton, this change meant the loss of huge numbers of people who had formed a part of the communities that the Parish served.

Furthermore, the loss of farming workers and their families coupled with the loss of the Hydro towns and their populations was even further compounded by the loss of those who had taken up soldier settlement farms after the Second World War. These farms (as elsewhere in Australia) were too small to be viable and eventually nearly every soldier settlement farm in the Central Highlands was bought out and taken over by surrounding farming properties, as Molly explains:

> There were more people living and working here … and there were a lot more dairy – and the reason being that from Ouse to Hamilton there were small dairy farms from the cut up of land for returned soldiers. So those people all had three or four or five children and so that made huge numbers in this area. Then as those places weren't sustainable and the children all went away at high school and a lot of them didn't want to be dairy farmers, or farmers, so there are very few of them at all still around in the area. They have moved on and the parents have retired away to Hobart or wherever.
>
> So, as a property, a dairy farm, came up for sale a neighbour would buy it and they'd become bigger. Then when that didn't work there'd be another sale. So, … it's only a very few properties now. So all these people have gone. Where there were, I think something like 20 something small dairy farms scattered around between Hamilton and Ouse and the roads off, now there would be two. (Molly, writer)

Another town in the district that the Parish of Hamilton serves is Maydena. This town had a large population in the order of several thousand people who were largely employed to log the surrounding forests for paper production at the paper mill located down-stream on the River Derwent at New Norfolk. Throughout the 1960's and 1970's right up to the present time, this paper mill downsized its work force due to increasing efficiencies resulting from mechanization at the mill and, therefore, the number of people required for logging also decreased and Maydena subsequently lost most of its population.

There is a marked grouping of a number of demographic and social factors that have specifically affected the Hamilton district, and consequently also the church: reduction in the number of families living and working on farms, the Hydro towns, settler farms, and logging for the New Norfolk paper mill. These factors all contributed to significant structural changes in society that eventually resulted in, after initial marked rises in population, a continuing decline in population and therefore associated services. Molly comments on this in terms of the number of schools in the area:

> So all of those people … still needed a workman, so they would have had children. So the school was booming and all these little areas had their own schools. Hamilton had a school. Wayatinah had a school. Tarraleah had a school. Bronte Park had a school. Ellendale had a school. (Molly, writer)

The change is not just in population; there has also been significant cultural change in the region. Mary comments, with a clear feeling of loss for the past and how things used to be, on this changed attitude to church and religion in the post-war years that impacted on local parishes in the Hamilton area, as elsewhere in Australia:

> I think the soldier settler blocks that started in this area after the Second World War and the men came back, it brought a different group of people into the area. A lot of young men who went off to the war felt that they'd missed their childhood; missed their teenage years; missed the fun of immediate post-school years. So they seemed determined to give their young that chance and I suppose a lot of us felt that they actually were quite spoilt. So, the discipline that had existed in the area prior to that seemed to begin to diminish and I think this is where our way of life changed. (Mary, retired)

The church had always been the centre of the community. However, this situation changed dramatically after the Second World War. The advent of significant cultural and social change in the post-war period (such as change in social organization, changes to work, religion, age profile, and family profile) saw the church becoming increasingly irrelevant to the lives of those who returned from the Second World War and for their children, too. Mary observes the effect of these changes on the local church:

> Well, the younger ones weren't very interested in coming to church. They would come Christmas and Easter – and they made their lives away from the area as well. Colleges were the thing; university was the thing; so they moved away. And a lot of them who'd been to church schools said, which I felt was always just an excuse, that they were *over*-churched. They weren't going to do that anymore. They were sick of being involved. (Mary, retired)

Other factors were also impacting negatively on the district and, therefore, on the Parish as well. Namely, environmental changes were being experienced in the area. Previously viable properties were unable to sustain stock or crops to the degree they had been able to do so formerly. Farms which were reliant on credit to sustain them through tough times were being stretched further and further and, as Mary's comments indicate, eventually many properties could not sustain the level of debt any longer and the banks foreclosed on their mortgages:

> And then we were in the period where the banks were being fairly ruthless with farming properties. We had severe drought, it was very difficult and, even though we felt we'd kept faith with the bank, in retrospect maybe there were other things we could have done, but we lost the property and that was a very tough scenario. (Mary, retired)

Further to this, the structure of world markets was changing and commodity prices fell rapidly. Many farms became economically unviable as working farms. They were sold to people who used them as hobby farms or weekend retreats. Often these new-comers came from Sydney or another 'mainland' city and they were able to purchase an historic colonial homestead in which to live for a fraction of the cost that they would have had to pay in Sydney or elsewhere. Many of these people did not live permanently in the district and this had an effect on the local shops, schools, hospital, and church. As Mary's quote indicates, many people felt the knock-on effect in the district of declining utilization of these services and infrastructure:

> But things were changing. Shops closed, shops changed ... even the sort of things they kept. When I was first married you could actually buy everything you needed at the local shop, even material to make children's clothes and the needles and cottons and everything else. I had no need to go any further. The local hospital, my babies weren't born there but you could still have your babies there. (Mary, retired)

The few working farms left in the district now tend to be farmed by a husband and wife team who are often aged in their sixties or seventies. Their children, who have typically attended university and are working in other professions, do not want to work on the family farm as they can see how physically and emotionally demanding it is and what little financial return there is for this effort. These farms are usually asset rich but cash poor; that is, the only real worth of the farm is, in fact, in the value of the land, the stock, the equipment, and the buildings and these are not able to be realized whilst the farm remains a working farm. This has had a profound effect on the Parish, as Mary explains:

> And the people that had once supported the church financially, very handsomely every year, usually the farmers – the money wasn't there any longer. And drought and the properties just weren't making the money that they used to make. I mean, the wool bale used to be ... a wool bale set aside was a very good contribution to the stipend. Well, that was no longer the case and nobody could afford to do it. We used to... everybody used to keep a heifer or something for sale. That beast would be set aside; that was money for the church. No longer could we afford to do it. It sounds incredible but ... we were living hand to mouth, most of the big properties. And so there was no longer the money to pay for a rector. And I think all of us quite happily go on continuing to give … time and many other little things but there's no longer a way that we can write a cheque for x thousands of dollars at the beginning of the financial year and say that's our commitment to the church. (Mary, retired)

Another major demographic factor is the trend whereby grown-up children leave the district. Molly describes two forms this can take where children of the husband and wife team sell the property to realize the asset after their parents have died or are too old to work the farm any longer or simply choose to live elsewhere:

> In recent times there have been farms either being leased out … our neighbours, they had two daughters and a son. That property now is leased because their son decided to stay in Hobart. He's got a wonderful job so that's just life. Whereas we always imagined, in the end, he might come home. Then a neighbour at the other end of the property had two daughters and a son and we assumed that perhaps that – and the husband died very early and that property now is half sold and they retained the other half. Just a small part with the homestead. So they're one each side of us. So, that's just one example, or two examples. (Molly, writer)

This trend is typical of many rural farming areas in Tasmania, and elsewhere. Such communities, and their parishes, have not experienced the demographic changes occurring in other rural areas and parishes in

Tasmania, such as New Norfolk or Channel/Cygnet or St Helens, where there has been an increase in the population. This continuing decline in population and services is a very 'heavy' situation for the residents/ parishioners to deal with – and very sad for these once thriving parishes within once thriving rural farming communities.

The history of population loss within the Municipality of the Central Highlands since the Second World War has been steady and unrelenting with the net effect of the loss of over two-thirds of the municipalities' population since the Second World War. Given this loss of population and the resultant loss of job opportunities the district now has a significantly older population and continues to experience population decrease. This has all impacted negatively upon the Parish of Hamilton and, despite various fund-raising efforts by parishioners, in 2002 the Parish could no longer afford the services of a full-time stipendiary priest.

Perhaps the final negative impact on the Parish of Hamilton, on top of the already negative impacts of demographic changes such as population decline and an aging population and cultural changes such as people choosing not to belong to the local church, occurred when a former priest of the Parish was charged with and convicted of child sexual abuse, including the abuse of children in parishes throughout Tasmania. The impact this had in the wider community and upon the parishioners and the Parish itself was devastating. In terms of the credibility of the church, this tragic occurrence was profoundly negative. Dealing with the consequences of such tragedy, in addition to the impact of major demographic and cultural changes, has been an onerous and demanding, and deeply distressing task. The local community as a whole is now wary of men holding positions in which they exercise pastoral and liturgical responsibilities. Interestingly, it is noteworthy that all Team members in the Parish of Hamilton are female.

The Parish of Hamilton is, in many ways, almost a 'worst-case' scenario in terms of how bad it can get for a rural parish. It is hard to imagine how it could have been any worse. And this has continued into the present day, where recent long-term droughts have seen farms become less productive and has required the shooting of live-stock due to lack of feed. Suicides on farms in this area reflect the untold story of the desperation still facing many farmers today in this farming community. Yet, despite all this, this

Parish is also an encouraging example of how, from very bruised, battered, depleted, and hurting things new things grow.

Options for the Future

The options facing the Parish, given all these factors and issues, were limited. The Parish had already been amalgamated several times over with neighbouring parishes. Given that further amalgamation with neighbouring parishes was not an option, the prospect of requiring a priest to serve this vast geographical area on a part-time stipend was deemed to be unrealistic. The various fund-raising initiatives (including the sale of the last rectory, the other rectories having all been previously sold) all proved unsuccessful in the long-term. There was a general consensus of opinion among the parishioners regarding the need to do something, but exactly what they didn't know, as Nicole explains:

> There was … an option for some sort of part-time or locum or just something like that. We tried locums that take services but they were just that. Just a blow-in/blow-out sort thing. We realised that would never be satisfactory in that – well, every man's only got two hands. He couldn't cope with the parish work and another parish as well. It was just a sort of general – I won't say despair – you know, a general, well what *are* we going to do? (Nicole, writer)

Therefore, the Parish began to explore the possibility of becoming an Enabler Supported Ministry parish. Public meetings were held in which ESM was explained and in which discussion could take place. It is reflective of the close ties between the Parish and the wider community that these meetings were all public meetings. Just as historically in the Central Highlands district leading members of the community were also leading members of the Parish, this is still in evidence today. As with the other communities of faith examined in this study, there were concerns about ESM, what it would entail, how it would work, and what it would mean. Many of these concerns centred on the feeling that people who had no training would be effectively running the Parish, as Mary explains:

> Well, I think it was probably the fact that it would be untrained people running the Parish and I think that's where those who did have a deep church background were probably most concerned. I think all of us were concerned that we could do it properly. However,

> how ever willing we were, were we going to be able to cope with it? (Mary, retired)

A great deal had been learnt from other parishes in the Diocese who had explored and implemented ESM. So, the process was far more fine-tuned than it had been for New Norfolk. During this exploratory phase, the Team and some parishioners from the Parish of St Helens visited the Hamilton Parish for a weekend to talk about ESM. This sense of collegiality, friendship, and willingness to help other parishes exploring ESM has been a hallmark of the way that ESM parishes look beyond their parish boundaries to care for others, offer assistance, share their experiences, and act as mentors.

This nurturing aspect of the ESM process validates the concerns, questions, and doubts of parishioners providing a forum and process for exploration and discussion. The concerns of the Hamilton parishioners were taken seriously and many meetings were held during which ESM was explained, as both Mary and Amelia recall:

> And … [they] came and talked to us … which I think clarified a great many things for *all* of us. Made us go away and think a lot more positively about things. (Mary, retired)

> There was a lot of talk.... There were a lot of meetings, a lot of discussion.… But I just think that slowly, slowly, there was a lot of paperwork given to us to read. Some of us did a lot of studies together that this paperwork had…. There was no hurry. There was no rush. And I think that's a really important part of the process. (Amelia, business proprietor)

One area that was reassuring to the parishioners was knowing they would have an Enabler to provide adequate training and guidance to the Team members, as Mary explains:

> And then, knowing that we were going to have you, James, as Enabler, I think gave us a lot of confidence; feeling that we weren't going to be on our own. That we would have a certain training; there would be somebody to ring up and say, "What do I do?" For all of us I think it's been a huge learning curve in a great many respects. I think the Parish has accepted us amazingly well, actually. (Mary, retired)

Team members also found themselves undertaking things that previously they would not have even considered:

> And I think I was fortunate enough to go off and do a CPE [Clinical Pastoral Education] course. I had no idea what I was letting myself in for but that was a very special time for me. Something that I would never have even thought about doing, probably. (Mary, retired)

> Well, I can remember leading the first service. Was I nervous! And preaching! Oh, I never thought I'd do that. (Nicole, writer)

The members of the Team 'called out' in the Hamilton Parish were representative of the demographic make-up of the area, as is the case in the other parishes. In the Hamilton Parish, this means the Team members are predominantly locals who were born in the area and have lived there all their lives or who have moved into the area decades ago. This composition of the Team has remained consistent, even though there have been some changes in Team members over the years.

After a year of exploration, examination, and training the Parish and Local Ministry Support Team (LMST) were Commissioned as an ESM parish on the 22nd of February, 2004. The work of the LMST has been well received within the Parish and by those in the wider community. There is also the recognition that there are advantages in the incumbent being a Team in terms of pastoral care and servicing such a large geographical area. Mary explains how effective this model is in terms of providing care that suits individual needs:

> Well, it's been a very special thing for me. I think the Team is a wonderful thing because … one person is not trying to deal with everybody; that there will always be people who don't want to deal with one person…. We know somebody probably will not want you sitting beside their bed or whatever so you ask somebody else to do it. And this is very important. And you accept that there are people who won't want you there and will ask for somebody else. That's how it should be.

> I think … when it comes to death and dying, or a family drama that is really serious, people will choose whom they would like to open up to and I think that maybe if there's only one person and they don't feel happy about that person, then that problem of theirs goes untended and I think that is dreadful. Whereas with four or six of us being able to do it there'll always be somebody, hopefully, that they will feel they can ring or write to or whatever they want to do or stop you in the street and say, "Have you got time?" (Mary, retired)

The Role of the Enabler

We will now outline how the role of the Enabler, which has been developed elsewhere in other ESM parishes, was implemented at Hamilton (see Chapter One for discussions concerning the theology of Enabling). Some people make the assumption that ESM is all about doing away with stipendiary ministerial support altogether. This is not the case at all. Others think that when ESM is up and running the Enabler's time required in the parish will be reduced. This is far from the reality of how ESM functions.

The ESM model of church requires that there be an Enabler for as long as the parish functions as an ESM parish and at the highest possible level of deployment the parish can afford. Of course, ESM moves a parish away from a pattern of dependency on the stipendiary priest and from the need to provide a full stipend, but the idea is not to replace it with a pattern of independence. Total independence of ministering communities is inconsistent with the Anglican pattern of ministry. Rather, in ESM, the ethos is to seek to build a healthy interdependence between the parish and the diocese. Therefore, the basis of ESM is to hold the local and the wider church dimension together in a healthy tension. All the gifts necessary to be church are believed to be present in the local context and, with the on-going support provided by the diocese through the Enabler, those gifts are identified, called, utilized, and continuously developed.

The stipendiary Enabler provides on-going education, formation, training, evaluation, and mentoring. In addition to being the key link person with the wider church, the Enabler is present in the parish as the theological educator and trainer for ministry drawing on her or his own formal education and training for ministry and experience in the church. Theological education and training for ministry remain a high priority following the Commissioning services and remain so into the future.

The Enabler is therefore essential to this way of being church. An ESM parish without an Enabler is not possible in the Anglican Church. The Parish Administration Ordinance (revised), which was approved by the Synod in 2002, legislated for both the place of ESM within the Diocese and for the role of the Enabler within ESM parishes (see Appendix 4).

In Enabler Supported Ministry, the role of the stipendiary priest shifts from that of being the primary leader of the church who does the bulk of the ministry for and to the people to one that enables the development of local leaders and the ministry of the whole congregation. In this way of being church, the ministry development task involves not only the education and training of the Local Ministry Support Team members and authorized local lay ministers but also of the entire congregation for adult Christian responsibility in the church and world.

The role of the Enabler is significantly different from that of the resident parish priest. The Enabler is responsible for the oversight of several parishes embracing a number of worship centres, congregations, and communities. Rev Collins prepared the following outline of the role of the Enabler for use amongst ESM parishes and also for parishes in the Diocese which are considering becoming an ESM parish:

The Enabler will not be:

- the dispenser of sacraments who travels at great speed from church to church every Sunday.
- the Parish administrator
- the key decision-maker without whom nothing happens
- the only preacher and minister of the Word
- the pastoral worker and counsellor regularly visiting and caring for the faithful
- the church's outreach worker, evangelist and community minister
- the one who disciples new Christians
- the performer of the rites of passage

Instead the Enabler will be:

- a facilitator of ministry and mission
- one who trains the laity for the work of ministry, helping to establish a pattern of every member ministry
- the developer of parish leaders and Local Ministry Support Teams
- a motivator and encourager of local community outreach to the wider community enabling local leaders to mobilize the congregation for mission
- a consultant who helps parishes evaluate mission strategies and develop plans

- one who networks parishes together encouraging a sharing of resources and building a sense of solidarity and common purpose
- someone with the skills of conflict resolution

The role of an Enabler is a demanding one. The Enabler needs to be able to work creatively and freely within a new framework and pattern of ministry. He or she will need to have a thorough grasp of collaborative ways of working. The Enabler will also have the ability to motivate and inspire people and be skilled in the management of change and in conflict situations. He or she will be someone used to working in partnership with others, rather than working alone in an isolated model of leadership. The latter skill is particularly difficult for many priests who, whether by training or inclination (or a combination of both), are steeped in the ethos of headship. The ESM concepts of sharing with others and training others to perform the duties of the incumbent feel to such priests not 'right'. Thus, Enablers need to be carefully selected and trained because the model is very different to traditional models where the parish revolves around the priest.

The Enabler is appointed by the Bishop and the Diocesan Ministry Council in conversation with the parishes involved. The appointment process is not the same as that of a rector or priest in charge. There is no Nomination Committee. The decision to appoint is made by the Bishop after conversation with the parishes and the Diocesan Director of Ministry Support who will have had an opportunity to meet the candidate(s) and assess their suitability.

The best way to view the Enabler is as a member of the Bishop's staff team whose services are 'purchased' by the parish in order to develop and maintain this way of being church. The line of accountability is to the Diocesan Director of Ministry Support and Bishop. Evaluation of the Enabler's ministry role is provided through the Diocese on an on-going basis.

The Enabler and the LMST

The Local Ministry Support Team at Hamilton, like most other LMST's, meets weekly with their Enabler for training, planning, and mutual support. In addition, the Enabler meets regularly with each Team member individually for training, mentoring, and advice and encouragement. The Team value this on-going training and support as they, along with the Parish Council, are responsible for the running of the Parish and, in particular, for the pastoral and liturgical life of the Parish. This pastoral role extends over the entire district and can involve driving over one hundred kilometres to visit people. In other words, as the following quotes from Mary and Amelia indicate, the Team takes their responsibility very seriously, but do so in an awareness that although they may not be 'perfect' they are committed to being there for those in need:

> A Ministry Team is a team which is set up to care for God's interest in this place and to lead the church. It is a responsibility.... I think the leadership Team has a responsibility for the nuts and bolts of the Parish and to set, make sure things flow, and there's always someone there. But the other side of the leadership Team is to walk beside all those within the worshipping community, to be their friend and to travel the road with them. Sharing the journey. (Amelia, business proprietor)

> People will accept our shortcomings. We don't have to be perfect. And I think the strength of being able to ring somebody up and say, "I have just had to do so and so", and the support, particularly for funerals and, obviously, when you live in a small area you're going to usually know the people for whom you're performing that last rite. It's difficult, but it's also amazingly special that you can do this thing for them. And that it is done absolutely as perfectly as you can do it and suitable for that person. (Mary, retired)

The demographic and cultural change that has impacted negatively upon the Parish of Hamilton has had an even more devastating impact upon all other church groups in the district. The Anglican Church is the only church group who still have a presence across the municipality and, therefore, the members of the Team are often having to care for members of other churches too as there are no other priests or ministers in the area. The Team accepts this responsibility and ensures that everyone in the district is cared for, irrespective of these people's church affiliation or lack thereof.

As the following quotes from Mary and Molly indicate, this acceptance of the work of the Team extends to members of other churches being willing to accept Holy Communion from the female Ordained Team Member (OTM) who is a part of the Local Ministry Support Team:

> Well in my eyes they're all God's people and really I have not been knocked back for want of a better term by any Catholic person and

> they have taken [part in] our services, come to our services when we have them at the hospital and they have accepted communion from Mavis and that's been a wonderful thing. And she's a woman priest and has been very well accepted in the area. (Mary, retired)

> So, church is beyond the walls of the building. So really, I think we have to walk among the people and if we can help them, we help them. I don't think – I would never, ever try to suggest to someone, "Oh you should be coming to church", because if they asked me I would say, "Yes, come on Sunday because I'll be there and I'll sit with you or talk to you". But I think it's something that's got to be choice. (Molly, writer)

The outward expression of mission and care shown by the Hamilton Parish Team does not necessarily result in any direct benefit to the Parish, but is an expression of the living out of their faith in the service of others. In other words, the model of church ministry facilitated by ESM allows the Team (and church) to connect with and enrich the lives of those in their local community without any expectation that such people will come to church. This is an example of non-proselytizing mission to the wider community that, while disregarded by those who adhere to proselytizing as a method of increasing church attendance and money, is an expression of service to others as service and care only. In the case of the Hamilton Parish, where historically there is a strong link between the community and the Parish, ESM has enabled a strengthening and extension of existing links between the community of faith and the wider community.

The care which the Team members have for everyone stems from their desire to care for others and this desire is enabled by the training they receive. This desire to reach out to care for those in need also, perhaps, stems from their own lived experience. As the following quote from Mary indicates, each Team member has experienced 'trauma' in his or her own life:

> I find it very interesting that each member of our Team has, in their own life, had to endure tremendous trauma. And I think this shows because the care is absolutely there and it's not emotional in the sense of it bringing up your own trauma, but, in our case, we went through a dreadful time and yet people were so good to us. And I think, then, you need to give it back. And if you've had a charmed life and everything's gone swimmingly, you don't know any of this.

> You don't *know* any of the depth and I think one should perhaps be grateful for trauma, if that's the case, that we do, we grow with it but then we know that other people in trauma need to have what you've been given. (Mary, retired)

This care that the Parish and the Local Ministry Support Team have for everyone in the district extends to advocating on behalf of the district itself. This has been most evident as the Parish has often been responsible for initiatives either to sustain existing services or to get new services for the well-being of the wider community. For example, the substantial community newspaper, *The Highland Digest*, is edited solely by a Team Member. This newspaper is not in any way a church paper, even a pseudo church paper, but a community newspaper for the whole of the Central Highlands district.

In addition, as the quotes from Mary and Nicole indicate, the effort to sustain the services provided by the local hospital located in Ouse was led by members of the Parish and, though it has not been entirely successful, saw the community come together as never before to 'save our hospital':

> Well, the Parish has supported it very fully. I would say that every member of the Parish has had some part in it. Some more than others. Along with the rest of the community. It's not a church thing by any manner of means. Some of the Parish members are on the committee. A lot of the Parish members have been on the hospital auxiliary for years, supporting it and visiting the people in the hospital and that sort of thing. The church is – well, I don't know if they see us as the church, but there's no doubt about it, that the church members in both Hamilton and Ouse are a hundred per cent involved in the fight for the hospital. (Nicole, writer)

> And those who are not necessarily members of the Team, but who have joined forces to help us fight to keep *something* in the area, whatever it may be.... And I think if we... even if we lose, we've got to feel that we've walked down every avenue. (Mary, retired)

The fight to prevent the closure of the Ouse Hospital consumed a great deal of time and energy and as Mary explains, they just kept on fighting because

> every time new information comes to us, like perhaps you could do this or perhaps you could do that, we keep thinking, "It's *not* dead in the water. *Something* has got to happen." (Mary, retired)

What inspired members of the Team and Parish to keep struggling to keep the hospital open was a deep and profound sense of care and compassion for their fellow residents of the district. This was a struggle to help people such as Mary describes:

> [The hospital] has a residential component. I think that was very neatly said by an older member of the community at our public rally in Hobart when she said, "I have no children and no extended family. All my friends are here and I had expected to end my days here." That was all she said. She didn't *need* to say anything else. (Mary, retired)

The concern in the community about the possible closure of the hospital is another example of the unrelenting withdrawal of government infrastructure and services in the district and the changes in social organization and culture. The Parish continues fighting to keep services in the Central Highlands area for the sake of the local population. Even though this is often not successful, there is a commitment to keep struggling to persuade authorities that people matter:

> I know in my own life of faith I have just ... my prayers have been full of how do you get people who are just full of ambition to understand that that's not everything. (Mary, retired)

For those in the Team and Parish of Hamilton their connection to the community is based on a theology of service. Thus, while the relationship between the faith community and the wider community is of a social and cultural nature it is, nevertheless, grounded in basic Christian theological principles of the servant and service. ESM, as a model of church that facilitates an 'elective affinity' between social and cultural context and the faith position of the church enables theological thought to manifest as social action.

Conclusion

In the municipal district of the Central Highlands, where the Parish of Hamilton is located, there has been, and will continue to be, significant population loss, aging of the remaining population, high unemployment, along with the withdrawal of government infrastructure and services. These factors have had an inevitable and significant effect on the Parish. It is a remarkable testimony to the resilience, creativity, and sheer hard-work of the people of the Parish and of the region that they have achieved all that they have. However, there will be long-term pressure on the Parish given the projections of the continuing decline and aging of the region's population. This pressure is real and there is a cost to those who are called to leadership within this context. Despite this, however, there is still a determination within the Parish to continue to care for all in the community.

Whilst ever they can continue to care for one another and all people in the district and whilst ever they can continue to gather for worship the people of the Parish of Hamilton will do so. As Gwen's comments indicate, they feel that they could do with help, though, and they will need to receive the on-going support of an Enabler who understands their particular social context:

> I think the Diocese needs to look at and become – we're actually a small place at this moment and, as I said before, I think the Diocese needs to take hold of itself, realize we're regional and rural, only a percentage of Tasmania and there needs to be far greater support coming out … I think (pause) for the Enabler Supported Team having the Enabler … I mean there's no way it would have worked without that. It needed, and it needs to have that person, needs to have that outside person coming in to keep it going ... that's just a reality of a small community. So it's always going to need that outside person. (Gwen, business proprietor)

At times it feels to the parishioners as though the Diocese does not understand what it means to be a very small rural parish in Tasmania and they sometimes feel the Diocesan hierarchy are "constantly undermining the energies and the faith" (Gwen business proprietor) of parishes in these isolated rural areas.

The Parish of Hamilton has tried unsuccessfully to secure small grants from the Diocese: for example, to support chaplaincy in the local schools (both primary and high school) and to fund a kitchen for Parish catering of community events. These applications for money in the region of $2,000 – $5,000 have been refused by the Diocese. However, there are Diocesan budgets (Anglican Church of Australia, Missionary Diocese of Tasmania 2010) in the region of $200,000 – $300,000 (increasing to $365,360 for the 2010/2011 financial year budget) for the Imagine Project to carry out its mission of evangelizing Tasmanians through such initiatives as a horse-riding venture, a 'church plant', a university student ministry, and the funding of one assistant bishop.

Despite this failure to achieve financial support from the Diocese for its out-reach and community-based activities, the Parish of Hamilton has maintained its support of school chaplains and is also involved in many community projects. This includes community projects that are outside the Parish of Hamilton. For example, with the New Norfolk Parish they provide assistance in Hobart for refugees recently settled in Tasmania, particularly help with teaching refugee women sewing and cooking using foods available in Tasmania.

The prosperity gospel that underpins the 'purpose driven church' intent on raising church attendance and offertory money and attracting children and having youth groups fails to acknowledge the reality of demographics and cultural change impacting on rural parishes in Tasmania. Such emphasis on youth, numbers, and money also fails to appreciate that there is value in very small congregations who are aging. ESM is a model of church that does allow for social and cultural context and the valuing of people's gifts. ESM, then, allows for the God of little things and little people. Big things do grow from little things, but it may be that some have such pre-conceived notions of what constitutes 'big' that they fail to appreciate some 'big things' when they see them. That is, what is achieved by parishioners in parishes such as Hamilton may seem to some in the church to be very little efforts by a little group of people but they are actually staggering achievements from a small committed group of faithful Anglicans who happen to live in a rural community.

The changed form of church structure that is ESM has allowed the community of faith to engage with the social and cultural changes in the area. The resilience of the community of faith to continue to engage in this process of change is evident in that, after a recent Calling Out, a new member of the Local Ministry Support Team was Commissioned on the 5th of July, 2009. This gives hope for a sustainable future for the Parish. In addition, another person has recently been 'called out' by the Parish to serve on the LMST and is currently undergoing a Diocesan discernment process prior to being commissioned.

Ammerman (2001) emphasizes that the future of parishes is dependent on them adding to the social and spiritual capital of the wider community in which they are set thereby contributing to the well-being of the wider community. The engagement of the Parish of Hamilton with the wider community contributes to the health and well-being of members of both the community of faith and the wider community. In the midst of massive cultural and social change smallness and the ability to cope with change and adapt are the greatest strengths for any parish or church (Drane 2001). In the Hamilton Parish, this is admirably reflected in the story of their journey over recent years as an ESM parish.

A Chronology of Events

1st July 1984: Parish commemorates the 150th anniversary of the laying of the foundation stone at St. Peter's, Hamilton.

1998: the Diocese appoints a priest (Claude) as the Diocesan Ministry Officer (1998-2002).

May 2002: The Diocesan Ministry Officer (Claude) leaves the Diocese.

December 2002: last full-time stipendiary Rector leaves Parish.

March 2003: Parish holds a vote to become an Enabler Supported Ministry Parish.

1st August 2003: James Collins begins as Enabler to Parish.

August 2003: a Local Ministry Support Team formed and begins to meet fortnightly.

22nd February 2004: Full Commissioning of Parish of Hamilton including the Commissioning of the Local Ministry Support Team (Jean Hayes, Mary Downie, Libby Shoobridge and Charlotte Pitt) and the Ordination to the Diaconate of those Called to Ordained ministry in the Parish (Ellen Clark and Martin Woolley).

9th July 2008: James Collins resigns as Enabler to the Parish Hamilton

5th July 2009: Wendy McCrossin Commissioned as a member of the Local Ministry Support Team.

Chapter Six: Theological Reflection

Introduction

The research about the four rural Anglican communities of faith in this book, while ethnographic, crosses the boundary between sociology and theology. This intersection arises from both the subject of the research, a cultural group holding a particular religious belief system, and because ESM itself facilitates an interrelatedness between the parish and its belief system and their social and cultural contexts. The four parishes have a sustainable future, each in their own contexts, even though other models and ways of being of church have not been able to achieve this sustainability. This stems from the inductive nature of the theology underpinning ESM that is sociologically informed and leads to the parishes expressing an outward focus, in which they engage with their context in a way that seeks the well-being of the wider community in addition to their own well-being. Such a focus is quite different to the focus in the parishes prior to the introduction of ESM, where they were primarily concerned with internal issues such as raising the finances to pay for the stipendiary priest. The quality of life and care within the community of faith of one person for the other is also enriched where this inductive, sociologically informed theological orientation is manifest.

The ethos underlying ESM is characterized by an incarnational theology (a theology that is grounded in the reality of the church's context) that resonates with vulnerability, by a church organization that supports and encourages mutual ministry and an emphasis on social justice and service, and by a sociology that fosters community participation and an engagement with post-modernity. Together, these characteristics lead to a model of church in which those exercising ministry within the parish, both Team members and parishioners, are committed to 'journeying with' rather than a 'leading of' other parishioners as well as those from the wider community. Most particularly, this 'journeying with' characterizes the role of the Enabler in the parish in terms of the relationship between the Enabler and Team members, and also with members of the parish. This relational ethos is rather beautifully described by Donovan (1982: vii), though in a different context, but equally applicable to ESM:

> [D]o not try to call them back to where they were, and do not try to call them to where you are, as beautiful as that place might seem to you. You must have the courage to go with them to a place that neither you nor they have ever been before.

This chapter discusses the sociologically informed theological basis of ESM in terms of the process of re-invention it facilitates, the issue of fundamentalism, and the issues of privilege and non-privilege. It then explores what an inductive approach means in terms of being church and the characteristics of a sociologically informed theology. The role of the Enabler to 'walk with' a parish seems, on one level, to be something of an uncertain journey. It requires a stepping out in faith to determine a direction for the living out of the Christian faith in new ways and in ways that are contextually and theologically grounded. Rev James Collins' experience as Enabler to the four parishes reveals this 'journeying with' and the need for both himself, as Enabler, and the parishioners in each parish to set off on a journey "to a place that neither ... [I] nor they have ever been before" (Donovan 1982: vii).

Process of Re-Invention

Upon arriving in Tasmania in 2001, it seemed to Rev Collins that it would be a good idea to get an understanding of the history of the State and of the Diocese. Therefore, apart from reading various books about Tasmania in general, he found a copy of the history of the Diocese of Tasmania marking the sesquicentenary of the Diocese in 1992 (Stephens 1991).

Stephens' history (1991) of the Diocese is as interesting as it is depressing to read, but is valuable for the historical insight it offers in terms of a background to parishes in the Diocese of Tasmania. From its founding in 1842 it would seem that there have been a number of tensions marking the life of the Diocese: tensions that remain to this day. The first of these tensions involves the divide between the North of the State and the South of the State. This divide would seem to impact on the Diocese as much as it does upon the State. One possible origin of this tension is the divide between 'free settler' in the North and 'convict settler' in the South. This divide, whatever its origins, remains a palpable reality in Tasmania. Stephens (1991) refers to three other tensions that have also historically impacted on the Diocese of Tasmania: the divide between urban and rural, between evangelical and anglo-catholic, and between the laity and clergy. The latter three tensions are not particular to Tasmania and would be familiar in the histories of churches in other parts of Australia and around the world.

These various tensions, to a greater or lesser extent, can still be seen today in the Diocese of Tasmania. While in many ways perhaps irrelevant to the day-by-day life of each of the parishes, these tensions are, nevertheless, a backdrop to the life and experience of these four rural parishes. In addition, and more specifically relevant today are the significant and on-going social and cultural changes beginning in the post-Second World War period that each of these parishes has experienced. In comments, in another context, made by Bauman and May (2007: 178) about change being like a stream can be seen this on-going change and the need to engage with this change:

> Just think of whirls in a stream. Each one looks as if it possesses a steady shape and so remains the same over a protracted period of time. Yet (as we know) it cannot retain a single molecule of water for more than a few seconds and so its substance remains in a permanent state of flux.

This process of engaging with on-going change requires creativity and imagination, along with hard work. There is a temptation amongst some communities (and this includes communities of faith) to

> seek to freeze the whirl, to bar unwelcome input into the knowledge they control and attempt to seal the 'form of life' over which they wish to secure a monopoly. (Bauman & May 2001: 179)

The Enabler Supported Ministry parishes examined in the case studies have sought to engage in a process of re-invention and have done so by moving from an inward focus (raising a stipend to sustain a stipendiary priest) to an outward focus by seeking the welfare of those with whom they share their lives. Their real concern for the 'other' (including those outside the parish) contributes to their health as churches. That is, an outward focus leads to inner health. A Biblical reference which highlights this change in focus is to be found in Jeremiah 29:7 which states that a community of faith is to "seek the welfare of the city where I have sent you ... and pray to the Lord on its behalf, for in its welfare you will find your welfare".

Each of the four rural Anglican communities of faith have this ethos of seeking the well-being of others in the wider community at the core of their life as is indicated from the following comments made by one parishioner:

> The clear and recent example is the agreement by the Parish Council to donate $8,000 over three years to a Chaplaincy Programme at Woodbridge School, which really, in terms of an immediate benefit to the Parish, … will be none. It's a generous gesture of seeking to build the kingdom of God in means other than the attractional model of bringing people along to church. Putting a Chaplain in the school and hoping … that person will, in some way, bring the grace of God into the school and into the lives of children who perhaps otherwise don't rub up against it too often. I mean a few years ago, that would have been totally out of the question. Well, I guess not only financially, but the mindset would never have allowed giving away $8,000. If there was $8,000 it would have to have been invested for the future because of the level of anxiety giving all that [money] away. (Sally, student)

Like the other ESM parishes, the Parish of Channel/Cygnet declares itself to be a "Church who have Christ at the heart of our lives and seek to bring the love of Christ to the heart of our community" (Anglican Parish of Channel/Cygnet, weekly pew-sheet, 25-6-2006). This echoes Küng's (1983: 486) words that the

> sign of a true vocation is not a miracle, but service for the benefit of the community. Any kind of ministry in the Church therefore is of its nature dependent on solidarity, on collegial agreement, on discussion among partners, on communication and dialogue.

While the term 'community' can be employed with a variety of meanings, nevertheless, community participation "may be understood as emerging in a community of place, generally involving collective actions, to undertake activities that are at some level perceived to be of benefit to the community" (Taylor, Wilkinson & Cheers 2006: 45). This is demonstrated in the life of the Teams as they work together for the well-being, not only of their parishes but also of their wider communities.

There has, however, been some critique of the 'team' approach utilized by business. One aspect of the 'Disneyization' of work is that of 'emotional labour' which requires the employee to consider their work as fun: that is, that they are not really working (Lyon 2002). Another critique of teams can be found in an article by Ezzy (2001) examining the individual and workplace community in which he takes issue with the use of 'team' as being very authoritarian. Likewise, Cowdell (2004: 221), whilst valuing a collaborative approach to work, questions the notion that "'the team' was an obviously superior category. Because, as we know, so-called 'teamwork' too often means no more than being individually disempowered, or else grouped together to do what we're told". The experience of the Local Ministry Support Teams is quite the opposite. In the interviews undertaken for this research the Team members themselves do not describe membership of the Team as being anything other than a positive experience (even given the demands that it makes on them).

A major demand on Team members is time: a balance is needed between the time a Team member has available and the demands of parishioners and those from the wider community on that Team member. Given that each Team member is a 'volunteer' and that they are not entitled to remuneration, other than re-imbursement for expenses as required by the Diocesan legislation (see Appendix 3, sections 6.c and 8), and that they each have homes, families, and often work, then the issue of time/availability is a significant factor in the life of each Team member. A Team member describes these ineluctable realities in the following way:

> I think [one] of the difficulties ... [is] that the Parish is limited by the amount of time that people have because most people on the Team, and certainly everybody in the Parish, have a busy life. A lot of people work, and so their ministry can't be their only focus of life, so there is a limiting factor in terms of time. I think that's true in other places as well. So sometimes I think that means that people's ministries can't necessarily be as fully developed as they would otherwise be. When we went into Enabler Supported Ministry one of the catch-cries was that we weren't going to clutter people up with meetings but, in reality, probably the majority of the Team members ... well, all the Team members meet weekly and run services regularly and most are on Parish Council and various other groups. So, that does mop up a fair bit of time just in the maintaining the status quo kind of meeting. So, the time for thinking ahead and planning and innovation and all the rest of it is a little limited. But, having said that, people will go above and beyond the call in so many ways. (Sue, teacher)

Team ministry is not just another leadership strategy but, rather, an expression of the worth of each participant. There is a radical equality that exists between members of the Team, despite their diversity and differences. Each Team member contributes to the whole in a deliberative process where each Team member is recognized and affirmed for who they are, and not just for what they achieve. This recognition of the worth of each person applies also within the whole community of faith and, equally, to the whole community, too. In other words, Team ministry affirms that the process is more important than the outcome and the life within the Team articulates and models what the nature and character of relationships outside of the Team might also be.

The Teams, in particular, and the parishes, in general, have sought to be particularly attentive to the context in which they are located and to respond to that context in ways that reflect the issues that are of concern to the wider community. The opposite position of assuming the Teams and parishes know what is best for the wider community would be an imposition of their will on the wider community. In a world of 'pre-emptive' military action whereby the agenda of the powerful is foisted on the weak, it seems only a slight shift in emphasis to talk about 'purpose driven churches' (churches that are grounded in their own reality). This can translate as someone (often male) discerning some particular purpose that they then use to 'drive' the church.

A spirituality that can remain vulnerable, as God is vulnerable, (Placher 1994) is a core principle of ESM. Likewise, ESM is based on a spirituality that listens rather than imposes, and which does not rely on having to find purpose but which is able to search for meaning amongst the bewildering perplexity of contemporary life. In addition, ESM encourages an awareness of the extraordinary sense of God's presence in that lack of purpose. This results in a spirituality that not only resonates for Rev. James Collins personally but that, amongst competing notions and claims as to knowing and understanding God's will, is more consistent with the life of the one to whom Christians attribute divinity. This is the one (Jesus Christ) who demonstrates that divinity is not inconsistent with the struggles, the joys, and the life that we are all called to engage in by virtue of our humanity – a humanity that, nonetheless, is infused with the divine.

The parishes studied have achieved a re-invention of themselves because they have lived out with integrity, consistency, and compassion a spirituality that is grounded in their shared humanity with other people. This living out of their Christian faith demonstrates their belief in a God who is vulnerable and compassionate. Because of its ethos, ESM promotes and supports these parishioners to live fully as human beings with a sense of the presence of the divine being manifest in their care for others and in their service of others.

Fundamentalism

The rise of various fundamentalisms around the world constitutes an aspect of the cultural context impacting on the four parishes, as well as churches world-wide. Fundamentalism represents one of the major ideological, political, and religious phenomena in contemporary society. It presents itself in various ways and through various movements, so that it is impossible to define fundamentalism absolutely. However, it is possible to discuss some of the defining aspects of fundamentalism. The discussion deals more with the underlying essence of fundamentalism than with the variety of ways in which it manifests itself in contemporary society.

Fundamentalism, in its various forms, is a world-wide phenomenon, and is now very much a part of contemporary life (Lyon 2002, Marty & Appleby 1991, 1993a, 1993b, 1994, 1995). The term 'fundamentalism' is perhaps an inadequate one to cover the diversity of issues covered under the broad umbrella of groups and ideologies that get labelled fundamentalist. Furthermore, the groups that are so labelled would, on the whole, generally prefer to call themselves 'conservative'; that is, they hold on to some perceived tradition that they consider themselves to be the defenders of. This is what Manji (2004: 150) calls "foundamentalism". On the other hand, they might see themselves as 'radical' (Manji 2004) or "aggressively impositional" (Pratt 2006: 1) because they feel that their message (or ideology/teaching/programme) is, in fact, counter-cultural. That is, they see themselves as offering a critique of existing structures and beliefs that, if adopted, would provide a solution to the 'ills' of contemporary society.

While no single definition of fundamentalism sufficiently covers the range and the diversity of forms in which fundamentalism appears it could, however, perhaps, be said that fundamentalism represents an attitude. It is a "movement which stresses the authority and literal application of its founding tenets" (Delbridge 1990: 714). It is interesting that the above definition prefaces the quoted sentence by referring particularly (and solely) to religious fundamentalism, and even more particularly to Christian fundamentalism. Such a narrow definition reflects the common misapprehension and misunderstanding of the nature of fundamentalism; there is a misconceived sense that fundamentalism is a religious phenomenon in general, and a Christian phenomenon in particular. It also fails to deal adequately with the variety of political and ideological groups that are fundamentalist in nature. Such a misunderstanding is common to most standard reference works. For instance, in *A Concise Dictionary of Theology* (O'Collins & Farrugia 1991: 82) fundamentalism is defined as:

> A movement in twentieth-century Protestantism, especially in the U.S.A., which generally defends such fundamental beliefs as the divinity of Christ and his bodily resurrection but interprets the Bible with little attention to its historical formation, various literary forms and original meaning. This neglect of good exegesis has led to false problems about such OT stories as creation, the flood and the story of Jonah.

As useful as this definition is with reference to Christian fundamentalism it, nonetheless, fails to mention other religions, or to expand the definition to include political and ideological forms of fundamentalism. Therefore, a broader definition is required which takes into account the underlying nature of fundamentalism in all of its forms as representing a particular attitude based on certain foundational tenets.

Even outside of the religious context, fundamentalism has about it a basic attitude that maintains that there is one correct view of life (proved beyond doubt by the particular founder or texts or ideas of the group) and that to right the wrongs of society, for example, this teaching should be followed absolutely by everyone.

This attitude is understandable, in part, given the complexity of contemporary society and the pluralism that results from this complexity. However, such an attitude tends to result in a 'guru' mentality, whereby a charismatic leader is able to persuade followers of the rightness of 'the cause'. In addition, there is often a sense in the group that the guru deserves absolute authority from followers, and that with the guru one does not discuss issues – one listens, learns, and serves. Furthermore, fundamentalist groups tend to become sectarian, both intellectually and organizationally, because of the strong pressure exerted on members of the group to conform and abide by the precepts of the leader and the hierarchy. Psychologically speaking, fundamentalism has a strong appeal to those who need to be right, to those looking for simple answers to the complexities of contemporary life, or to those who like to be dependent on someone else to tell them what to do or think or believe.

This sectarian outlook then tends towards a fortress mentality where engagement with the world is seen as evil because one becomes contaminated by the forces outside. The fortress mentality is one side of the coin; the other is the holy war mentality where the external world needs to be shown the truth, even by force, for their own good. Fundamentalism can also transform from non-dangerous to dangerous. Pratt (2006: 1) observes that fundamentalism

> denotes … a shift in mentality from the relative harmlessness of an otherwise quaint, ultra-conservative … religious belief system; to a religiously motivated and fanatically followed engagement in aggressively impositional, even terrorising, activity.

In contemporary society, there is as much scepticism as there is credulity. People are sceptical about bureaucratic organizations (be they religious, political, or ideological); yet, there is an enormous amount of credulity towards many groups or gurus who purport to know the truth. Such groups or gurus expound the uncompromising view that if one wants to be free then one only needs to follow this group or guru. Fundamentalism will always figure prominently in such contexts. Fundamentalist ideology tends to result in a misconception that believing a particular tenet will result in freedom or salvation.

As Macquarrie (1972) suggests, behind this misconception is a profound confusion between faith and belief:

> [T]he church has encouraged this misconception by laying an undue emphasis on correctness of belief and making this the primary criterion of its membership.... But faith is something more inclusive than belief. It is a total attitude toward life, and although belief is a part of this attitude, its essence is to be seen rather in commitment to a way of life. (27-28)

Ultimately though, fundamentalism may not, and in many cases does not, satisfy people's deepest desire for meaning in their lives as the meaning fundamentalism gives is one that is imposed, not freely chosen. There is a need for fundamentalists to be uncompromising because they think such rigidity suits their interests and purposes best (Barr 1981, 1984). In the troubled contemporary world, fundamentalism is "an enduring and emblematic feature of life" (Huff 2008: 161), but it is very dangerous due to its lack of tolerance and respect and the diminishing place accorded to reason (Bruce 2000, Carnley 2004, Schultz 2005).

The communities of faith examined in this study have all experienced significant decline and associated financial problems. Often in such situations, churches tend to become conservative, insular, and inward-looking: they can become fundamentalist in some sense. However, in the case of these four parishes, as is clearly in evidence in Chapters Two to Five, the opposite has occurred; that is, the parishes display an outward and inclusive engagement with their wider communities, and they are anything but fundamentalist. They see their mission to be one of service, not exclusion or condemnation or imposition. Their understanding of mission is in line with the 'Five Marks of Mission' developed by the world-wide communion of the Anglican Church (*The Anglican Communion Official Website*) that emphasizes loving service, justice for all, and care of creation.

It is encouraging to see this inclusive understanding of mission being incorporated into many Anglican churches in Australia. In the four parishes it is clearly evident that they pursue such an inclusive missional approach to their wider communities in their various activities of service and care. Their outward focus on care leads not only to health in their parishes but also to health in their wider communities. In other words, this outward focus on others leads to an inner health.

Privileged and Non-Privileged

Another insight into corporate religious life is provided by Weber (1965: 97, 95) who, in his analysis of the religion of non-privileged classes in *The Sociology of Religion*, draws a distinction between the religion of the middle class which he considered "inclines in the direction of a rational ethical religion" and the religion of the non-privileged classes where "we encounter an apparent increase in the diversity of religious attitudes". Weber (1965) sees the middle class adopting an attitude based on their distinctive being, whereas the non-privileged classes adopt an attitude based on what they will one day become. This singular difference in attitude leads to another attitude that is then adopted by the middle class who see their privilege (in politics, economic status, health, love, or anything else) as being earned by them. The non-privileged classes, on the other hand, see themselves in an altogether different light; that is, they see themselves as being unable to attain the status of the privileged because of their ontological difference. In other words, because the privileged are good, they are blessed; because the non-privileged are not good, they are cursed (Weber 1965, 1976). All that remains for the non-privileged is to hope for either a retribution to take place in this world, or the next, so that their suffering in this world may be ameliorated. This desire or hope for just compensation is, of course, a vain one for the privileged tend not to forgo their privilege. Resentment and the hope of a future compensation tend to go hand in hand (Weber 1965).

Further to this, Mannheim (Abercrombie, Hill & Turner 1988), following Marx, extended the concept of privileged and non-privileged classes beyond religion to encompass socio-political considerations as well. For Mannheim (Abercrombie, Hill & Turner 1988: 262), the beliefs of the subordinate classes "emphasized those aspects of society which pointed to the future collapse of the established order".

These concepts of 'privileged' and 'non-privileged' are useful for the discussions of the four communities of faith. In two senses, they belong to the non-privileged group. Firstly, within the Church structure they have, at most, very limited power because authority is vested in the controlling church hierarchy. Secondly, in their wider communities they tend to largely occupy a marginal position in that they exercise little or no authority or power in the functioning or decision-making of those wider communities. As such, they have a broader range of options available to them that they can consult (such as ESM) because they are not so constrained as are the 'privileged' groups in the Church or the wider community. Further, as a 'non-privileged' group they are more likely to pursue possibilities and options considered 'other', if not anarchic, than are 'privileged' groups, such as those found within the traditional Church hierarchy who have vested interests in maintaining the status quo.

The four parishes engage with their contexts in such a way as to seek the well-being of the wider community and not to overthrow, or seek the destruction of the communities in which they are set. Because of the sociologically informed theology that underpins the ethos of ESM, these parishes, whilst having a 'non-privileged' status, are concerned with engaging with and caring for the wider community. Further, it might be the case that having lost so much that defined these communities of faith in terms of power, privilege, and prestige (largely to do with financial status) that their 'non-privileged' status has allowed them to think creatively about their future and to engage in a dialogue with the wider community. Dialogue between parishioners, as Ammerman (2001) discusses of the US context but that is also applicable to the Tasmanian context, is a crucial aspect of the health of parishes and is encouraged by the ESM model of being church.

The 'non-privileged', then, in their disempowerment or lack of power are actually blessed because they can consider alternative ways of being, if they choose to, and dialogue is the primary means of exploring such alternative models of church. Radcliffe (2005), in his book on contemporary Christianity, devotes several chapters to the importance of conversation between those of differing views. Tracy (1994: 20) has also written on the need for dialogue:

> Conversation in its primary form is an exploration of possibilities in the search for truth. In following the track of any question, we must allow for difference and otherness. At the same time, as the question takes over, we notice that to attend to the other as other, the different as different, is also to understand the different as possible.

The role of dialogue is of the utmost importance in the life of the four rural Anglican communities of faith. An important part of the development of Enabler Supported Ministry in any parish includes a 'listening exercise' that helps the parishes come to understand their social and cultural context. This facilitates what Tracy (1994: 20) describes as the ability to "attend to the other as other, the different as different, [and] also to understand the different as possible".

Despite their 'non-privileged' status, the four communities of faith examined in the case studies have entered into an on-going dialogue between themselves and with their wider community. In so doing, they have contributed to the social and spiritual capital of their faith communities and their wider communities.

An Inductive Approach

An approach to engagement with the context in which they are located is a defining characteristic of the ESM parishes. This type of engagement with context is based on an inductive approach to socio-historical understanding (Cowdell 2004). This is different to other parishes that operate from either a deductive or reductive approach. In the inductive approach, the ordinary things of life are able to be invested with a meaning that transcends their very ordinariness because inductive theology is grounded in context. Berger (1969: x) sees ways of pointing "toward the reality beyond the ordinary" in his notion of the 'signals of transcendence'. Berger (1986: 232) considers this theological approach as inductive

> *not* in the sense of modern scientific method, but in the sense of taking ordinary human experience as its starting point.... Using more conventional Christian language, I might say that my approach is 'sacramental' – an apprehension of God's presence 'in, with and under' the elements of common human experience.

Berger considered that there are three different methodologies for understanding religious truth in contemporary Western society:

> The first, he terms 'deduction.' It involves reaffirmation of the authority of a religious tradition, in spite of the difficulties of doing so in the context of modern pluralism and within the assumptions of socio-historical relativism.... He labels the second method 'reduction' and ... [h]ere the religious tradition is reinterpreted via modern, secular categories in the hope of making aspects of the tradition meaningful to the modernist mind. The last method, 'induction,' involves an attempt to uncover and retrieve essential experiences embodied in the religious tradition. It is both empirical and comparative, in that it takes all religious experience seriously in its search for transcendent reality. (Gaede 1986: 170)

This study draws on this understanding of religion and of society and the forces that shape and affect it. The four parishes are examples of an inductive theology in practice that is grounded in context. This demonstrates how a particular contemporary expression of religion (Anglican) using an alternative model of being church (ESM) has relevance to the wider community (contemporary Western society), even given secularization and pluralism.

The value in Berger's approach to religion is that he takes everyday life as a starting point for an approach to religion based on 'induction', "which, if systematized theoretically, would lead to an inductive type of theology" (Zijderveld 1986: 74). ESM embodies this approach to religion based on 'induction'. Hence, it fosters a theology that is inductive and open to context. In turn, following Weber (1976), we suggest that ESM, because of this inductive, sociologically informed theology, has been effective in shaping the social organization and action of the four parishes in response to social and cultural change.

This research project is based upon sociological theory and provides an analysis of the lived experience and the social and cultural context of those within the four rural Anglican communities of faith in Tasmania. However, by virtue of the methodology chosen for the project, namely ethnography and participatory action research, there is a dialectic relationship between understanding (that is, description and analysis) and policy/action. Therefore, this project is also beneficial in demonstrating how alternative models of being church (in this case, ESM) can bring new life to struggling and declining churches and to the wider communities in which they are located.

A Sociologically Informed Theology

In contemporary Western society, theology needs to be relevant and one way of achieving this is to infuse theological understanding with sociological understanding. Bouma (2006: 168) maintains that there is a link between theology and sociology:

> Theologies not only describe the ideal or expected relationships between the transcendent – usually given personal features – and humans; they also more or less explicitly describe the ideal relations among humans and groups in a society.

ESM is an example of what we describe as a Weberian 'elective affinity' that is concerned with relationship. This 'elective affinity' can be seen in two ways: there is an 'elective affinity' between ESM and the post-modern Western world, and ESM itself fosters an 'elective affinity' between the ideas, beliefs, and actions of the parishioners and their cultural and social contexts. This is a relationship that is characterized by compatibility and support, which theologically reflects the relationship manifest in the Trinity.

> Between the persons of the Trinity there exists unity in diversity and diversity in unity. Therefore, rather than using the doctrine of the Trinity as a tool and/or weapon to exclude alternative view-points, the doctrine itself provides a conceptual framework in which we might recognize rival definitions of reality, without necessarily having to view them as being in competition with each other for a share of the 'market' (Berger 1967, Carnley 2004, Wuthnow *et al.* 1984).

Bouma (2006: 168), in his discussions of the interconnectedness between theology and sociology, emphasises the relationship between the human and the divine:

> God's relationships with Godself, with creation and with humanity will be expressed using images and concepts shaped by believers' experiences with human relationships. This goes beyond psychology; it is social because of the three persons in relationship. Thus, each theology presupposes and gives expression to sociology of the divine–human relationship.

The doctrine of the Trinity, although it can be used as a means for defining orthodoxy, can also be used as a doctrine that allows for an orthopraxis without having to take an adversarial view regarding 'rival definitions' (Berger 1967, Carnley 2004, Wuthnow *et al.* 1984). This orthopraxis, whilst not doing away with theological rigour, focuses on the lived experience of the person and/or community as being of primary importance. Furthermore, the doctrine of the Trinity highlights the relational nature of God. God is a relational Being: both between the persons of the Trinity and between the persons of the Trinity and humanity and all creation.

In the contemporary Western world, rather than being in a position of power the church is required to re-evaluate the role that it can play in society. Given the pluralistic situation in which the church finds itself, and also given the fact that the church has significantly less power than it held in former centuries, a theology of service has re-emerged as being an authentic expression of the churches' true nature and role within society. As one example of this, ESM is an alternative model of being church that encourages service and promotes relationship. In the four parishes can be found examples of this inclusive service to all and the emphasis on relationship with those within the church community of faith and with those in the wider community.

A theology of service is based on the model of Jesus, which not only affirms relationship but also values the richness and diversity of gifts in each person. Therefore, whilst the institutional church is seen by many in the West to be irrelevant, there is an authentic manifestation of the churches' true nature and role within society when, in service of others, it brings forth life, love, and being. This study has revealed that ESM, based as it is on a sociologically informed theology, is way of being church that facilitates an engagement with contemporary Western society in an attitude of relationship with and service to all people.

ESM: Sociologically Informed Theology in Practice

The research clearly demonstrates that discussions concerning the relationship between theology and sociology are more than just discussions about abstract theories: they are indicators of practical possibilities. That is, there is a combination of theory and practice. This dialectic relationship between theory and practice (praxis) allows for description and analysis as well as the capacity to transform ideas into action. This is clearly in evidence in ESM as it is practiced in the four parishes.

For the church to be able to embody a credible gospel (that is, both a message and a way of life) for the twenty-first century it must engage in the contexts in which it finds itself. This is as applicable for Tasmanian churches as it is for churches elsewhere in Australia and world-wide. Alongside this, there must be a conscious reuniting of social thought and action with theology and pastoral care, particularly at the local community level, rather than divorcing real life concerns from spiritual matters. Ministry models that perpetuate dependency (Dowie 1997) require re-thinking. Christians, regardless of their wealth, education, or status, need to be empowered and equipped to live their lives in line with the gospel, and to tell it to others with meaning. In this way, Christians can engage with contemporary society through the liberating gospel of Jesus Christ in ways that embody integrity, relevance, and meaningful relationships.

Rev James Collins' work as an Enabler, amongst other appointments, within the Anglican Diocese of Tasmania has involved serving these four rural Anglican communities of faith as they seek to be authentic manifestations of the relational, servant God, bringing about life, love, and being within the communities in which they are set. Telling the story of these four rural Anglican parishes as they live out this expansive and inclusive life, love, and being has formed the heart of this research; it is a story about this emerging, yet very fragile (fragile in terms of institutional power), new way of being church. One of the characteristics of institutional power is that it fails to take note of anything outside its organizational structure (Lyon 2002). In many ways, ESM is actually empowered because it is outside institutional power structures of the traditional church and is able to connect people to a theology of servant-hood.

These four rural Anglican communities of faith are expressions of the churches' nature and role within society that can arise when the church engages with context. Each of these parishes is located in rural Tasmania and, therefore, they are all concerned about the rural decline evident throughout Tasmania. Nevertheless, they seek to empower their wider local communities to be all that they can be by affirming the giftedness of those within each community. There is something radically egalitarian about these parishes; and the communities in which they are set are experiencing new hope as a result of the service which these communities of faith are offering their communities. Post-modernity opens up new possibilities for being church (Lyon 2002). ESM is a prime example of such 'new possibilities'.

In the four communities of faith, this new and inclusive way of being church is clearly manifest in four ways:

1. There is a recognition of all gifts that exist within the community. This recognition concerns the gifts of all people, rather than just some people. For example, traditionally the church acknowledged gifts in men for ordination but not women, which results in a system that has largely diminished the capacity for people to express their creativity or to receive recognition for their particular skills and attributes (Küng 2001). ESM promotes and supports a universal and egalitarian recognition of gifts, rejecting any recognition of gifts based solely on criteria such as gender. Such an ethos also results in shared leadership where the emphasis is on mutuality and relationship, not hierarchical dominance and control. The theology undergirding this practice forms a significant component of training both the Team members and parishioners, as Sally explains:

> But one of the good experiences in moving towards Enabler Supported Ministry was that quite a lot of effort and energy was put into the theology which underpinned it and so there was quite a lot of looking at various passages of scripture, particularly in regard to God as Trinity and the Trinitarian model of the peripatetic dance stepping forward, stepping back [and] there not being sort of permanent positions of dominance, that there was interaction. Also a lot of looking at the Corinthians' experience and the spiritual gifts. The 1 Peter thing, the royal priesthood. We did quite a lot of theological work. We did a lot of exploration of gifts and all that kind of stuff.... We actually put quite a lot of work and emphasis on that to try and understand how it would be. (Sally, student)

The praxis in ESM that facilitates an interaction between theory and practice enables recognition of social capital in all of its forms. This results in a perspective within the church affirming that all people are gifted. The relationship of mutuality between church and wider culture, as evidenced in full recognition of people's gifts, contributes to the diverse, yet relationally united, whole that makes for society in all its fullness (Cowdell 2004).

2. There is a recognition of diversity. Because giftedness is not restricted to any one gender, race, creed or nationality there is a possibility of lessening the focus on the adversarial view of 'rival definitions' so that we might simply acknowledge that there are different definitions of reality which can 'co-exist' with one another (Berger 1967, Carnley 2004, Lyon 2002, Wuthnow *et al.* 1984). In ESM, as it is practiced in the four parishes, there is a democratic character to the relationship between people and between view-points. Lola, from New Norfolk, sees this as a "ministering to the people by the people", which is not "just confined to church" but includes the whole wider community. Lola goes on to describe her view of the church as being an integral part of the community:

> It's not a 'them and us'. It's like it's an 'us'. Part of the 'us' doesn't always come to church to worship but that part of the 'us' is always reliant on the church, knows we're there, talks to us in the street. Every member has conversations with people and so it is, you know, still the body of the church in the community, but not every part of the body works the same way. (Lola, retired)

Therefore, the issue of how to relate to all people, whether they be church-goers or not, and how to express truth in this context of pluralism requires an openness to dialogue and to learning from others. The recognition of diversity denies the assumption that any one person or group has complete access to Truth (Drane 2001, Lyon 2002). Similarly, feminist theology and philosophy provides another conceptual framework that challenges the church not to limit the recognition of giftedness to only those who fit within particular socially defined roles (Hardesty 1987, Küng 2001).

3. There is a recognition of the centrality of relationship. These four communities of faith are able bring about life, love, and being for society through an emphasis on authentic relationships. Liberation theology provides a conceptual framework that challenges the church to be something other than an institution that exists for its own ends (ABC 1976, Bosch

2001, Brown 1990, Freire 1973, Gutierrez 1988). The connection with the wider community that is in evidence in each of the parishes reveals how the focus is on both themselves as church and on those outside the church in a relationship of mutuality, as Sally describes of Channel/Cygnet:

> There have been things like we've had music in the park, we've had peace gatherings and community events which ... have been organised by the church and from a Christian perspective but in such a way that they tap into a broader spirituality which is appealing to alternative lifestyle kind of people. There have been attempts in terms of art exhibitions and things like that. (Sally, student)

As God is relational, and as we see in Jesus the one who serves, the church is called, likewise, to serve and to be truly relational (Holloway 1997). The four parishes reveal this focus on service through relationship with each other and with those in their wider communities.

4. There is a recognition of the centrality of social justice issues. The four communities of faith have an expansive attitude towards others, and are concerned for social justice. Parishes can be effective advocates for social justice (Warner 1990). This social justice applies as much within the church as without, as the institutional church has often neglected issues to do with social justice (Boyce 2001). Throughout rural Tasmania, there is an increasing level of poverty and the four communities of faith seek to serve those who have no voice for themselves in a variety of ways as Sue and Mary outline:

> Links with the wider community in terms of pastoral links are fairly strong. The church is involved in Eating With Friends which is an outreach and friendship group for elderly folk linked in with the Community Health Centre with the RSL [Returned and Services League]. (Sue, teacher)

> I mean we recently had a working bee for a young couple. The husband has a very serious illness; he's in a wheelchair. They needed their garden done and they needed the approach to the house made suitable for wheelchair access and everything else. So there was a working bee and several of our church members went along to that and yes, again I would say that we don't have a group which is responsible for working bees or anything like that but if the need is

> there it quite often is met. A parishioner will ask for particular help to be given to someone and it will happen. (Mary, writer)

Likewise, the bureaucratic/institutional church which measures 'success' in terms of money and numbers fails to recognize that if this measure for success continues to be applied, the only areas that this measure will be applicable to will be in wealthy upper and middle class suburbs in the cities. The inclusiveness and expansiveness of God's life, love, and being demands that church be for all, not just for the rich (Lyon 2002). Such an inclusive attitude is clearly in evidence in the activities and programmes put on by the church for the wider community and in the assistance given to Rwandan refugees, as Louise describes:

> We've had family days at Snug where there were donkey rides and balloons and all sorts of things. Things were free. Sausages were actually given away, BBQ sausages, which a lot of the public couldn't understand. So we've had a day like that. There have been things in the park at Cygnet.... I know Fred is in with Rwandan refugees now. Jane has supported refugees.... I think more is being given to mission. I think we're becoming more of a giving parish. As long as we have enough to keep the electricity bill paid and things like that, we're giving a lot more money away. (Louise, retired)

A defining characteristic of the four communities of faith is their commitment to the service of others. Their out-reach activities are focussed on service to others as service only, and not as a way of increasing the number of people attending church.

In these four areas can be seen inclusivity in practice: these parishes do not merely talk about service and inclusivity – they put it into practice in real and concrete ways that arise from the context of their wider communities. Thus, in St Helens there is a 'furniture ministry' as this was perceived to be a need in the area; in Hamilton the church fought to keep the local hospital from being closed; in Channel/Cygnet support is given to Rwandan refugees; and in New Norfolk there is a commitment to ensuring the disabled have access to public buildings and to assisting with a settlement programme for newly arrived refugees. In ESM is a model of being church that unites theory and practice in the reality of social and cultural context and people's lived experience.

Conclusion: A Place That Neither I Nor They Have Ever Been Before

ESM is undergirded by an inductive, sociologically informed theology that encourages and empowers the practical expression of parishioners' commitment to live out the example given by Jesus in the reality (the social and cultural context) of these four parishes. There is an 'elective affinity' between ESM and post-modernity, and ESM facilitates an 'elective affinity' between the parishes and their current social and cultural contexts. As can be seen in the four parishes, a theology that is sociologically informed leads to an outward focus concerned with others, rather than an inward focus on themselves.

Other models, or ways, of being church might be appropriate in other contexts. However, the homologous relationship existing between ESM and the four rural Anglican communities of faith examined in the case studies, and their respective contexts, suggests that ESM is a way of being church that is situated within context, not in opposition to context. Adopting ESM is a journey that is not clear or pre-determined: it is worked out in process. As Enabler to these four parishes, Rev Collins has walked with them in a journey "to a place that neither … [I] nor they have ever been before" (Donovan 1982: vii). And the journey goes on.

Conclusion

Introduction

This book tells a story of four Anglican communities of faith in rural Tasmania. This story is important. A new model of church ministry (ESM) has enabled these four parishes (New Norfolk, Channel/Cygnet, St Helens, and Hamilton) to find a new future for themselves despite having been in serious decline for some time. It is an ethnography of hope because it reveals how ESM has facilitated an 'elective affinity' between the faith position of these parishes and their social and cultural contexts, bringing about an enrichment in the church and in the wider community.

In the contemporary Western world, Christian churches in many countries are facing serious decline and struggling to have relevance in people's lives. This study provides a worthwhile contribution to discussions about the place of the Anglican Church in the world today. While specific in terms of its focus on rural Anglican Tasmanian parishes, it is valuable for what it says about how small churches can be healthy and engaged with their wider communities. It also speaks about the value of 'small' in a world that tends to value only 'big', and in a Christian world where some opinion equates 'small' with 'failure' and 'big' with 'success'.

The Story We Tell

One of the motivations for this research is the sheer beauty and courage and graciousness of the people with whom Rev Collins works. The 'success' oriented church growth mentality sometimes looks on these people and parishes as "lame dogs" (this is an actual description by one of the younger clergy in this Diocese!). We take great heart from the fact that Jesus was not rich and successful. We think the problem with the 'purpose driven church' model is not that it is specifically concerned with numbers and money (increasing both of these), *per se*, but that it pursues this in disregard of social and cultural context. In addition, those supportive of the 'purpose driven church' model tend to focus on a restricted interpretation of the gospel that dismisses church models such as ESM as being barely Christian and as woefully inadequate; they do so because church models such as ESM express an outward expression of the gospel that focuses on service and care of all rather than on proselytizing and growth through raising money and numbers of attendees.

The ESM parishes have grown in confidence and knowledge of their capacity to engage with their communities as representatives of the Anglican Church. They have matured into a sense of knowing 'where they stand' within the hierarchical structure of the Anglican Church – they remain marginal in the life of the Diocese (that is, ESM is not the main focus of the Tasmanian Anglican Diocese). Nevertheless, these parishes are not fazed by the power and privilege that is vested in the hierarchy of the Anglican Church because they have experienced, beyond their expectations, the success of ESM.

While many (ourselves included) may be critical on theological grounds of church models that promote 'bigger is better' (in terms of the number of attendees and the money they give) we think the crucial point to be learnt about this 'success' oriented model of church is its 'isolationist policy'. This is why an ethnography, grounded in sociology rather than theology, can not only share the stories of these four parishes but also reveal one way of understanding why they are able to connect with and enrich not only their community of faith but also the wider community in which they are situated. This research has sought, as Geertz (1973) discusses, to think imaginatively with the people of these four parishes and to tell their stories in a way that makes their stories accessible to others and consultable by others. The ESM parishes of New Norfolk, Channel/Cygnet, St Helens, and Hamilton do not function as churches in isolation from their social and cultural contexts but are engaged with these contexts. The reason for this is that ESM facilitates an 'elective affinity' between their faith position (that is, their theological self-understanding) and the context in which they are situated (that is, the social and cultural context of the contemporary Western world as it exists in these rural parts of Tasmania). By undertaking a sociological research project that draws on a number of theorists such as Weber, Berger, and Drane, we have been able to explore the relationship between all these factors.

The study draws on over thirty interviews, demographic data for the municipalities in which these parishes are located, and Rev Collins' own knowledge and observations. The research reveals the value of parishes, which are facing difficulties due to widespread social and cultural changes, adopting a different model of church (ESM).

ESM had facilitated a power shift from a single stipendiary priest model to a Team/parish model, gender equality in terms of parishioner participation, inter-connectedness between parishioners and the wider community, and an organic structure focussed on well-being. This 'elective affinity' between parish and context has engendered an outward and inclusive orientation that contributes to the enrichment of both parish and wider community.

Rural Tasmania is as much affected by social and cultural changes as any community in Australia, whether urban or rural. Communication and information technology, a global economy, and the mobility of the Australian population all impact significantly on rural Tasmania. In Tasmania, there has been significant demographic change and there has been even greater cultural change. These social and cultural changes can be seen in the story of the four parishes.

The New Norfolk Parish story speaks of courage. As the first parish to commit to an exploration of ESM and to its implementation, the Parish of New Norfolk was the 'guinea pig' for the development of ESM in the Diocese. Therefore, there were no others parishes that they could look to for advice or help with regard to ESM. By adopting ESM, the Parish was able to move from despair about their future to hope for their future.

The story of the Channel/Cygnet Parish is one of transformation. Their story is a journey from door-knocking to raise money to pay for a stipendiary priest to being able to support Rwandan refugees and advocate on their behalf. In addition, their outward focus and connectedness with their wider community is evident in their concern for environmental and social justice issues.

The story of the Parish of St Helens (Break O'Day) is a story of service to others. Their story tells of movement from impending closure to the creation and running of a 'furniture ministry' to help the disadvantaged, not only in their wider community but also in communities further afield.

Finally, the story of the Parish of Hamilton is a story about resilience and the value of the 'small'. This Parish, because of its geographical location, is in an area characterized by inexorable decline in population, lack of employment, and reduction in community services. Yet, this Parish has achieved health as a very small parish that is committed to issues affecting their wider community, such as fighting to prevent the closure of the Ouse Hospital.

Together these four stories tell a story of ESM: of how ESM was able to facilitate hope, inclusivity, and courage to engage with an unknown future and to bring well-being to themselves and to their wider communities. The ordinariness and seeming similarity of the stories of these four communities of faith demonstrates that ESM has been an appropriate response in four different contexts. As such, they are not an isolated phenomenon, but are indicative of how an inductive, sociologically informed theology has facilitated a connectedness with the wider community. The result has been an enriching of the social and spiritual capital of both the parishes and their wider communities. That these ordinary people have managed to achieve this level of connectedness and care when other models of being church were unable to do this is a story worth telling. By seeking to care for their communities, they have also re-invigorated their parishes and this has led to a sustainable future for these four communities of faith as opposed to their neighbouring parishes that continue to struggle. This is the whole point of telling the story of what may, at first impression, look like ordinary people in ordinary situations, doing similar things. It is a story of relationship between parish and community and the underlying Weberian orientation of the study reveals that the church culture evident in these parishes (a theology that is inductive and open to context) shapes the social organization in, and the action of, these parishes.

These four parishes have enjoyed new life under ESM. However, it is important to note that these parishes are not somehow 'lucky examples'. They are parishes full of ordinary people facing the same difficulties and challenges as any in Tasmania face. Indeed, the strength of ESM as a flexible model of being church is borne out by the fact that none of these parishes has been immune to tragedy and loss and change. One parish lost its only Ordained Team member (priest) to an unexpected and sudden death, and a Team member in another parish was struck by personal tragedy. Key people have repeatedly left every one of these four parishes. In other words, ESM is a model that copes with 'real life' and is not dependent on things always going to a set plan and always working out as expected, and nor is it reliant on a few prominent people. In addition, three of the four parishes (New Norfolk, St Helens, Hamilton) are located in municipalities that are ranked (Vinson 2007) as being amongst the most disadvantaged in Tasmania.

This ethnographic story-telling, because it enables a close look at the stories of cultural groups, examines these parishes in relation to their social and cultural contexts. It also reveals the living out of their faith (as loving neighbour) and reveals the theological grounding/background of how these communities of faith understand themselves and their place and role in their wider communities. Parishioners' self-understanding (that is, their cultural/theological understandings) shapes how they live and make sense of life in their communities of faith. This ethnographic research is sophisticated storytelling that tells a story and reflects on the social and cultural context of the group that the story is about.

What the Story Tells

The story of this study is one of engagement, service, and relationship. It tells of church being church in its context, not in isolation from its context. It tells of ESM as being a way of church ministry that relates to its social and cultural settings and hence enriches both the parish and the wider community. ESM has allowed the parishioners in these parishes to hold onto the depths of their beliefs and traditions while at the same time engaging with the change and fluidity and diversity of a secular post-modern world. ESM enables the holding in tension of 'change' and 'non-change' because in being grounded (holding onto a theological foundation of belief) it allows for change in response to social and cultural context.

The homologous nature of ESM ensures flexibility and the ability to adapt as and when needed. Such adaptation, however, is not to such a point that parishes lose their Anglican tradition, but it is enough to cope with the changes, vagaries, complexities, difficulties, losses, and tragedies that life brings. ESM, then, is only ever a 'working blueprint', not a 'final blueprint', because it facilitates response to context and change, while holding on to the core beliefs and traditions of the Anglican Church. The emphasis is on the journey as opposed to the destination: on the process as opposed to the product.

As is so often the case in rural Tasmania the Anglican Church is frequently the last church of any description left in the communities in which they are set. Practical ecumenism is manifest through welcoming all people in the community to worship and through pastoral care of all in the community. However, this inward focus on gathering people for worship and caring for people forms only a part of the ethos of the four rural Anglican communities of faith that are examined in the case studies. Their outward orientation forms an equally significant part of their corporate life. It is this holding of the inward orientation and outward orientation together in a healthy tension that contributes to the sustainability of these communities of faith. Indeed, this is 'elective affinity' in practice, combining both sociological and theological process and insight. The story of these four parishes reveals ESM as a way of being church that facilitates a flourishing of the communities of faith and their wider communities. This is because of an 'outward' focus that engages with context rather than resists it, and that has shifted from a focus on raising money to a focus on others.

In the stipendiary priest model of church, the impact of social and cultural changes can result inadvertently in a tight focus on finances. While a certain level of money is required to sustain a parish (pay bills, upkeep of buildings, diocesan assessment, *etcetera*) ESM takes the financial pressure off the parish because a stipend is not required to support a priest. Although ESM parishes pay for the Enabler, the Enabler's work is located across a number of ESM parishes and this means that the Enabler's stipend is met from a number of parishes.

The Australian and Tasmanian context confronting Anglican churches is one where it "would appear that, economically, many parishes are finding it increasingly difficult to cover the full costs of the stipend and allowances of clergy" (Hughes 2001: 28). Hughes goes on to say that, given

> the age profile of congregations, the fact that in 1996, 24 per cent of all attenders on a typical Sunday were 70 years of age or over, and another 19 per cent were over 60, this situation is likely to worsen. In some rural areas, the problems of declining church attendance are compounded by declining population numbers. (Hughes 2001: 28)

Further to this, it "is likely that the numbers of clergy who can be employed full-time in the Anglican Church will fall rapidly in the next decade" (Hughes 2001: 28). The response to this situation that Hughes outlines, particularly in the rural context, has been to employ a range of responses that typically include amalgamation, fractional appointments, or supply clergy. On the whole, such responses are not successful, and, in addition, parishes have little or no sustainable or healthy life under such responses.

Rural communities in Tasmania were once very stable places, but now they are places of constant change, characterized by secularism and pluralism. This demands an outward looking resilience in the community of faith so they are able to engage with their community and the issues impacting on their community and to serve rather than to be served. The research reveals that, although embracing what is different (a different model of church) is a frightening prospect full of anxiety and uncertainty, it can, and does, lead to an enriched life. Courage is needed to embrace difference and different processes and different organizational structures; also needed is something akin to, following Bouma (Thornhill 1992: 172-173 cited by Bouma 2006: 2), "'a shy hope in the heart'". This mixture of hope and courage characterizes the four parishes as they opted to explore and commit to ESM. In terms of the problems facing many churches in Australia, as well as in contemporary Western society, it is important to acknowledge that change is difficult and requires a degree of hope in another way of being church, and that being 'outward looking' (as opposed to being only 'inward-looking' and focussed on raising money and numbers) is a necessary ethos to embrace for securing a sustainable future.

With reference to the four rural Anglican communities of faith in this study, their decision to become ESM parishes has brought a level of sustainability unknown since the Second World War. It is significant (and sobering) to draw a comparison with their neighbouring parishes.

The neighbouring parish to New Norfolk (apart from Hamilton) is Brighton. In the last decade the Parish of Brighton has had three part-time incumbents since the last full-time incumbent left over ten years ago and has experienced long gaps between each incumbency. This situation led to parishioners being concerned and uncertain about the viability of the Parish. After a long process of exploring options, the Parish of Brighton has now been commissioned as an Enabler Supported Ministry parish. The Parish of Brighton is already showing signs of renewed health as it turns its focus away from an inward focus on such things as raising a stipend to an outward focus on such things as supporting the local school chaplain.

In some situations, ESM may not be a feasible option due to the negative effects of long-term amalgamations that have been brought about by significant population loss, in particular. For example, the Parish of Southern Midlands, which abuts the Parish of Brighton, had reached such a low point of decline that ESM was not an option, and an alternative option had to be sought for this Parish. Thus, while ESM is a significantly valuable model of being church, it is not a 'miracle' model, and there are some places where it will be appropriate and others where it will not be appropriate. The important point is that some sort of alternative to existing traditional forms of being church based on stipendiary priests needs to be investigated for parishes struggling with long-term decline and financial and numerical unsustainability.

The neighbouring parish to Channel/Cygnet is Franklin/Esperance. Over the past decade, the Parish has also experienced a combination of part-time incumbents, with long gaps in between appointments. Although they have experienced decline and uncertainty they have nevertheless, chosen to pursue another part-time appointment. As indicated, ESM is not a 'top-down' model of church but one that is a 'grass-roots' model. Therefore, it is not something that can, or should, be imposed, but needs to be carefully considered, as is the case in the four parishes.

The neighbouring parish to St Helens (Break O'Day) is Dorset. In the last decade, the Parish of Dorset has had a number of part-time appointments and experienced long periods without any priest. Parishioners have been concerned for some time about their decline and viability into the future, compounded by significant on-going population decline and job losses in the district. The Parish of Dorset is currently exploring whether to become an Enabler Supported Ministry parish.

The four parishes reveal a high level of sustainability and connection to the wider community that is in contrast to many surrounding parishes. Given this what, then, is the measure of success for these four parishes? It is that these four rural Anglican communities of faith have come to a level of sustainability and, in the words of Ammerman (2001: 5), achieved a level of "survival as the institution determines it should be". That is, rather than being dependent on external support, such as supply clergy or fractional appointments, for their well-being they have achieved a level of autonomy that allows them to be self-sufficient and culturally and socially relevant in their local contexts.

Nevertheless, as a model of church ministry, ESM is very much characterized by team leadership that is under the guidance, training, and mentoring of an Enabler. This team ministry means that ministry is shared and "that a range of people take responsibility. It also means a larger range of gifts [are] being drawn on in the ministry of the church" (Hughes & Kunciunas 2009: 15). At a practical level, it is of crucial importance that developing, training, and supporting teams within the parishes/communities of faith are maintained. In the Tasmanian context, this is a very important initiative that is central to Rev Collins' work. Along with the willingness of these communities of faith to change, it is important, as Ammerman (2001) says of the situation in the United States, to have teams at a diocesan level who are prepared to support and walk with these people and parishes/communities of faith.

Finally, one of the most interesting aspects that the research has revealed in terms of the wider value and application of ESM is what this model of church can provide to more traditional models of church. As one of the interviewees commented, priests could learn a great deal from ESM in terms of ministry. We think one of the most valuable insights that ESM as a different way of being church can offer other types of church models is the ability to embrace change and engage with social and cultural context without losing the living out of the Christian faith. Indeed, the latter is enhanced by such engagement because it combines change with holding on to what is central to Christian belief – love and service of others without the expectation of people coming to church or of more money in the plate.

Conclusion

There is a lack of ethnographies of mainstream Christian groups, particularly Australian, and there are none of Anglican parishes in rural Australia. This study, then, fills a current void in ethnographic research. The story of four Tasmanian rural Anglican communities of faith, New Norfolk, Channel/Cygnet, St Helens, and Hamilton, is a story of hope. It is a story that tells of what happened when these four struggling parishes, faced with long-term decline, impoverished finances, and looming closure, opted to try a different way of being church, Enabler Supported Ministry. These are stories about ordinary people achieving extraordinary things.

These stories demonstrate that these four Parishes have achieved a sustainable way of being church given their social and cultural contexts. This success is something we can all learn from, not because these are spectacular successes (that is, 'big' in terms of money and numbers) but because they clearly demonstrate the quite remarkable successes that are possible when church engages with context.

Humans have always told stories. Stories, in whatever form they take (art, music, dance, spoken or written words), are the best means we have for understanding our world. We tell stories to convey something and also as a way of interpreting the story that is told. Ethnography is a particularly valuable sociological research methodology that allows for the telling of a story of a particular cultural group and for interpretation of, and reflection on, that story. The story told in this research is one of how these four rural

Anglican communities of faith have achieved sustainability through a change in church culture (to ESM). This alternative model of being church has as its foundational ethos an outward focus connected to community that results in practical benefits to parish and wider community.

These stories also represent the culmination of a journey begun in 1996 when the Diocese of Tasmania began exploring new and sustainable ways of being church given the social and cultural context of Tasmania. The Diocesan report, *Moving Out – Moving On* (Anglican Church of Australia, Diocese of Tasmania Viability and Restructuring Committee 1996), recognized the need for new models of church that were appropriate to context. It was also recognized that no one model of church would be suitable in every situation and recommended the development of team ministries in parishes. ESM, as developed in the four parishes, is a direct outcome of this report and has proved itself to be a model of church that facilitates sustainable churches with a capacity to engage with society.

Alternative models of church, such as ESM, enable the church to reach out into the community. In the future such alternative church models are the means by which churches will be able to regenerate themselves as communities of faith and to reach out into their communities, resulting in the enrichment of social and spiritual capital for both communities. "They will take with them the traditions of faith, but will build new communities of faith as new generations respond to God's Spirit" (Hughes & Kunciunas 2009: 15).

The four parishes stand as examples of taking models of church (in this case ESM in the Anglican Church) into the future that hold onto their traditions and beliefs but also change to suit particular social and cultural contexts. The value of these stories, then, is in demonstrating how this is achievable. The "consultable record" (Geertz 1973: 30) these stories provide is one of hope for the future that other struggling churches and parishes who are seeking to flourish and to engage with their context may be able to learn from.

May it be so.

Epilogue: The Parishes in 2016

Enabler Supported Ministry in Tasmania is in a mixed state in 2016. The absence of Enablers has left some parishes without Enabler support. Some parishes remain healthy, others are struggling.

Hamilton has ceased to be an Enabler Supported Ministry Parish. After key team members left the area, a Chaplain was appointed whose responsibilities include Hamilton. The parish remains very small but committed, with congregational attendance at the now fortnightly service varying from a low point of 2 to a high point of 30 at an Easter service.

New Norfolk is also moving away from being an Enabler Supported Ministry Parish. Although there is a strong ministry team, there have been extended periods where the ministry team has been without the support of an Enabler. In the absence of an Enabler, the Parish is now coming under the responsibility of a priest from a neighbouring parish. The numbers attending services have remained about the same with those moving away or dying being replaced by people who have moved to the area. They are actively involved in the community, visiting the local nursing home and hospital.

St Helens is still an Enabler Supported Ministry Parish. The ministry team has had some extended periods without the support of an Enabler. While there has been some decline, they still have good numbers attending their two services on Sunday, healthy finances, and strong engagement with the community. They feel well supported by the Diocese.

Channel/Cygnet remains an Enabler Supported Ministry Parish with a core of 5 to 6 active members, although these are all aging and no younger people are attending. They feel well supported by an Enabler.

Gwen's prescient comments more or less account for the current state of the four Parishes:

> We're actually a small place at this moment and … I think the Diocese needs to take hold of itself, realize we're regional and rural, only a percentage of Tasmania and there needs to be far greater support coming out … I think (pause) for the Enabler Supported Team having the Enabler … I mean there's no way it would have worked without that. It needed, and it needs to have that person, needs to have that outside person coming in to keep it going ... that's just a reality of a small community. So it's always going to need that outside person. (Gwen, business proprietor)

References

ABC (1976) *O Freedom! O Freedom!* Sydney: The Australian Broadcasting Commission.

Abercrombie, Nicholas, Stephen Hill and Bryan S. Turner (eds) (1988) *The Penguin Dictionary Of Sociology* London: Penguin Books.

Ackrill, J.L. (1973) *Aristotle's Ethics* London: Faber & Faber.

Ammerman, N.T. (1990) *Baptist Battles: Social Change and Religious Conflict in the Southern Baptist Convention* New Jersey: Rutgers University Press.

Ammerman, N.T. (1994) 'Telling Congregational Stories' *Review of Religious Research* 36 (4): 289-301.

Ammerman, N.T. (2001) *Congregation & Community* New Jersey: Rutgers University Press.

Anglican Church of Australia, Diocese of Tasmania (1999 [Amended 2000]) *Ministry Council Ordinance* Hobart: Diocese of Tasmania.

Anglican Church of Australia, Diocese of Tasmania, Viability and Restructuring Committee (1996) *Moving Out – Moving On* Hobart: Diocese of Tasmania.

Anglican Church of Australia, Missionary Diocese of Tasmania (2010) *Business Paper, Synod 2010* Hobart: Diocese of Tasmania.

Anglican Church of Australia Trust Corporation (1995) *A Prayer Book for Australia* Hong Kong: Broughton Books.

The Anglican Communion Official Website http://wwwanglicancommunion.org/ (accessed March 2005)

Australian Bureau of Statistics (1996) *Census Data.* http://www.abs.gov.au (accessed 2003-2004).

Australian Bureau of Statistics (2001) *Socio-Economic Indexes for Areas.* http://www.abs.gov.au (accessed 2003-2004).

Australian Bureau of Statistics (2002) *AusStats: Themes Tasmania Population in Municipalities.* http://www.abs.gov.au (accessed 2003-2004).

Australian Bureau of Statistics (2003) *Australian Social Trends* updated 3 June 2003, Economic resources - income distribution, Social Policy Research Centre. University of New South Wales, http://www.abs.gov.au (accessed 2003-2004).

Australian Bureau of Statistics (2006) *Census Data.* http://www.abs.gov.au (accessed 2008).

Barr, J. (1981) *Fundamentalism* London: SCM Press.

Barr, J. (1984) *Escaping from Fundamentalism* London: SCM Press.

Bauman, Z. and T. May (2001) *Thinking Sociologically* Oxford: Blackwell.

Bearup, G. (2003) 'Praise the Lord and pass the chequebook' *Good Weekend* 25 January: 14-18.

Beavan, E. (1988) *Take Heed Lest You Forget: A History of St Peter's Anglican Church Hamilton* Hamilton, Tasmania: St. Peter's Church Vestry.

Bentley, P., T. Blombery and P. Hughes (1992) *Faith Without the Church? Nominalism in Australian Christianity* Kew: Acorn Press Ltd.

Berger, P.L. (1967) *The Sacred Canopy: Elements of a Sociological Theory of Religion* Garden City, New York: Doubleday.

Berger, P.L. (1969) *A Rumour of Angels: Modern Society and the Rediscovery of the Supernatural* New York: Doubleday.

Berger, P.L. (1986) 'Epilogue' in J. Hunter and S. Ainlay (eds) *Making Sense of Modern Times: Peter L. Berger and the Vision of Interpretive Sociology* London: Routledge & Kegan Paul: 221-235.

Berger, P.L. (1992) *A Far Glory: The Quest for Faith in an Age of Credulity* New York: Free Press.

Berger, P.L. and T. Luckmann (1966) *The Social Construction of Reality* New York: Doubleday.

Bosch, D.J. (2001) *Transforming Mission: Paradigm Shifts in Theology of Mission* New York: Orbis Books.

Bouma, G. (2006) *Australian Soul: Religion and Spirituality in the Twenty-first Century* Cambridge: Cambridge University Press.

Boyce, J. (2001) *God's Own Country: The Anglican Church and Tasmanian Aborigines* Hobart: ISW.

Brain, P. (2009) 'Rural Towns and Cities' in S. Hale and A. Curnow (eds) *Facing the Future: Bishops Imagine a Different Church* Brunswick East: Acorn Press: 101-111.

Briggs, J. (2002) 'Do-it-yourself church delivers way ahead for rural parishes' *The Saturday Mercury*, 16 February, Hobart: News Limited: 5.

Brighton, W. (2004) *Attendance Statistics For the Anglican Church of*

Australia (1991-2001) Sydney: Standing Committee of General Synod.

Brown, R.M. (1990) *Gustavo Gutierrez: an introduction to liberation theology* Maryknoll: Orbis Books.

Bruce, S. (2000) *Fundamentalism* Cambridge: Polity Press.

Carnley, P. (2001) *Does Ministerial Priesthood Have a Future?* A sermon preached in St Martin's Church, 11 July, Hawksburn, in the Diocese of Melbourne. http://web.stpeters.org.au/views (accessed June, 2005).

Carnley, P. (2004) *Reflections in Glass: Trends and tensions in the contemporary Anglican Church* Sydney: HarperCollins.

Carroll, J. (2008) *Ego & Soul: The Modern West in Search of Meaning* Carlton North: Scribe Publications Pty Ltd.

Centenary Committee of St. Paul's Church, St. Helens (1983) *St. Paul's Anglican Church St. Helens: The first 100 years* St. Helens: Saunders Press.

Cowdell, S. (2004) *God's Next Big Thing: Discovering the Future Church* Mulgrave: John Garratt Publishing.

Cray, G. (2007) *Disciples & Citizens: A Vision for Distinctive Living* Nottingham: Inter-Varsity Press.

Davie, G. (1994) *Religion in Britain since 1945: Believing without Belonging* Oxford: Blackwell.

Davie, G. (2006) 'From obligation to consumption: Understanding the patterns of religion in Northern Europe' in S. Croft (ed) *The Future of the Parish System: Shaping the Church of England for the 21st Century* London: Church House Publishing: 33-45.

Delbridge, A. (ed) (1990) *The Macquarie Dictionary*, Second Revision, Macquarie University, New South Wales: The Macquarie Library Pty Ltd.

Dempsey, K. (1990) *Smalltown: A Study of Social Inequality, Cohesion and Belonging* Melbourne: Oxford University Press.

Dick, B. (1995) *You Want to do an Action Research Thesis?* Brisbane: Interchange.

Donovan, V. (1982) *Christianity Rediscovered* London: SCM Press.

Dowie, A. (1997) 'Resistance to Change in a Scottish Christian Congregation' *Scottish Journal of Religious Studies* 18 (2): 147-162.

Dowling, R. (1997) 'Baptism and Confirmation' in G. Varcoe (ed) *A Prayer Book for Australia: A Practical Commentary* Alexandria, NSW: E.J. Dwyer (Australia) Pty Ltd: 51-63.

Drane, J. (2001) *The McDonaldization of the Church: Spirituality, Creativity, and the Future of the Church* London: Darton, Longman and Todd.

Dunnill, J. (2001) 'Ministering Communities' in the New Testament' *St Mark's Review* 187 (4): 19-27.

Ellis, C. (1997) 'Evocative Autoethnography: Writing Emotionally About Our Lives' in W.G. Tierney and Y.S. Lincoln (eds) *Representation and the Text: Re-framing the Narrative Voice* Albany: State University of New York: 115-139.

Ezzy, D. (2001) 'A Simulacrum of Workplace Community: Individualism and Engineered Culture' *Sociology* 35 (3): 631-650.

Fichandler, Z. (2002) 'Creation Theory' *24 Hours*, September, Sydney: The Australian Broadcasting Commission: 32-33.

Finke, R., and Rodney S. (2000) *The Churching of America 1776-1990: winners and losers in our religious economy* New Brunswick, New Jersey: Rutgers University Press.

Frame, T. (2007) *Anglicans in Australia* Sydney: University of New South Wales Press Ltd.

Frankenberg, R. (1969) *Communities in Britain: Social Life in Town and Country* Middlesex: Penguin Books Ltd.

Freire, P. (1973) *Education for Critical Consciousness* New York: Seabury Press.

Frost, M. (2006) *Exiles: Living Missionally in a Post-Christian Culture* Massachusetts: Hendrickson Publishers, Inc.

Gaede, S. (1986) 'The problem of truth' in J. Hunter and S. Ainlay (eds) *Making Sense of Modern Times: Peter L. Berger and the Vision of Interpretive Sociology* London: Routledge & Kegan Paul: 159-175.

Geertz, C. (1973) *The Interpretation Of Cultures* New York: Basic Books.

Giles, K. (2002) *The Trinity and Subordinationism* Downers Grove: Inter-Varsity Press.

Gutierrez, G. (1988) *A Theology of Liberation*, 15th anniversary ed, rev.,

Maryknoll: Orbis Books.

Hale, S. and A. Curnow (eds) (2009) *Facing the Future: Bishops Imagine a Different Church* Brunswick East: Acorn Press.

Hardesty, N. (1987) *Inclusive Language in the Church* Atlanta: John Knox Press.

Harrower, J. (2004) *a healthy church transforming life* Hobart, Tasmania: Diocese of Tasmania.

Harrower, J. (2009) 'A New Openness to Change' in S. Hale and A. Curnow (eds) *Facing the Future: Bishops Imagine a Different Church* Brunswick East: Acorn Press: 203-212.

Heidegger, M. (1962) *Being and Time*, Translated by John Macquarrie and Edward Robinson, London: SCM Press.

Hilliard, D. (2002) 'Pluralism and New Alignments in Society and Church 1967 to the Present' in B. Kaye (ed) *Anglicanism In Australia: A History* Carlton South: Melbourne University Press: 124-148.

Holloway, R. (1997) *Dancing on the edge* London: Fount Paperbacks.

Holy Bible (1989) *New Revised Standard Version* Nashville, Tennessee: Thomas Nelson, Inc.

Huff, P.A. (2008) *What Are They Saying About Fundamentalisms?* New York: Paulist Press.

Hughes, P. (2001) *Working in the Anglican Church: Experiences of Female and Male Clergy* Kew: Christian Research Association.

Hughes, P. and A. Kunciunas (2009) *Models of Leadership and Organisation in Anglican Churches in Rural Australia* Kew: Christian Research Association.

Küng, H. (1980a) *Does God Exist?*, Translated by Edward Quinn, London: Fount Paperbacks.

Küng, H. (1980b) *Why Priests?*, Translated by John Cumming, London: Collins.

Küng, H. (1983) *On Being a Christian*, Translated by Edward Quinn, Suffolk: Fount Paperbacks.

Küng, H. (2001) *Women in Christianity*, Translated by John Bowden, London: Continuum.

Lohrey, A. (2005) *Voting for Jesus: Christianity and Politics in Australia*

Melbourne: Black Inc.

Lyon, D. (2002) *Jesus in Disneyland: Religion in Postmodern Times* Cambridge: Polity Press.

Macquarrie, J. (1972) *The Faith of the People of God* New York: Charles Scribner's Sons.

Macquarrie, J. (1977) *Principles of Christian Theology* London: S.C.M. Press Ltd.

Manji, I. (2004) *The Trouble with Islam* Sydney: Random House.

Marty, M. and R. S. Appleby (eds) (1991) *Fundamentalisms Observed* The Fundamentalism Project, Volume 1, Chicago: University of Chicago Press.

Marty, M. and R. S. Appleby (eds) (1993a) *Fundamentalisms and Society* The Fundamentalism Project, Volume 2, Chicago: University of Chicago Press.

Marty, M. and R. S. Appleby (eds) (1993b) *Fundamentalisms and the State* The Fundamentalisms Project, Volume 3, Chicago: University of Chicago Press.

Marty, M. and R. S. Appleby (eds) (1994) *Accounting for Fundamentalisms* The Fundamentalism Project, Volume 4, Chicago: University of Chicago Press.

Marty, M. and R. S. Appleby (eds) (1995) *Fundamentalisms Comprehended* The Fundamentalism Project, Volume 5, Chicago: University of Chicago Press.

National Church Life Survey (2001) *Executive Summary: Anglican Diocese of Tasmania* Sydney: National Church Life Survey Research.

National Church Life Survey (2006) *Executive Summary: Anglican Diocese of Tasmania* Sydney: National Church Life Survey Research.

O'Collins, G. and E.G. Farrugia (1991) *A Concise Dictionary of Theology* New Jersey: Paulist Press.

Pickard, S. (2009) *Theological Foundations for Collaborative Ministry* Surrey: Ashgate Publishing Limited.

Placher, W. (1994) *Narratives of a Vulnerable God: Christ, Theology, and Scripture* Louisville: Westminster John Knox Press.

Pratt, D. (2005) 'Religious Plurality, Referential Realism and Paradigms of

Pluralism' in A. Plaw (ed) *Frontiers of Diversity: Explorations in Contemporary Pluralism* Amsterdam: Rodopi: 191-209.

Pratt, D. (2006) 'Terrorism and Religious Fundamentalism: Prospects For a Predictive Paradigm' *Marburg Journal of Religion* 11 (1): 1-15. http://www.uni-marburg.de/fb03/ivk/mjr (accessed March 2008).

PurposeDriven http://www.purposedriven.com.au/pd_40dop_Overview.asp (accessed July 2006).

Putnam, R.D. (2000) *Bowling Alone: The Collapse and Revival of American Community* New York: Simon & Schuster.

Radcliffe, T. (2005) *What is the Point of Being a Christian?* New York: Burns & Oats.

Rwandan Coffee Club http://www.rwandancoffeeclub.org/index.html (accessed May 2007).

Reason, P. (1993) 'Reflections on sacred experience and sacred science' *Journal of Management Inquiry* 2 (3): 273-283.

Rice, P. and Ezzy, D. (1999) *Qualitative Research Methods: A Health Focus* South Melbourne: Oxford University Press.

Ritzer, G. (1996) 'The McDonaldization Thesis: is expansion inevitable?' *International Sociology* 11 (3): 291-308.

Schultz, J. (2005) 'The Ideology of Religion' in J. Schultz (ed) *The Lure of Fundamentalism*, Griffith Review, Sydney: ABC Books: 7-10.

Sherlock, C. (1997) 'The Ordinal' in G. Varcoe (ed) *A Prayer Book for Australia: A Practical Commentary* Alexandria, NSW: E.J. Dwyer (Australia) Pty Ltd: 148-157.

Simons, M. (2007) *Faith, Money and Power: What the Religious Revival Means for Politics* North Melbourne: Pluto Press Australia.

Sinden, G. (1978) *When We Meet for Worship* Adelaide: Lutheran Publishing House.

Sofield, L. and C. Juliano (2000) *Collaboration: Uniting Our Gifts in Ministry* Notre Dame: Ave Maria Press Inc.

Spong, J.S. (2001) *A New Christianity For a New World: why traditional faith is dying and how a new faith is being born* Pymble, NSW: HarperCollins.

Staudenmaier, J. (1988) 'Restoring the Lost Art' *The Way* 28 (4): 313-321.

Stephens, G. (1991) *The Anglican Church in Tasmania: A Diocesan History to Mark the Sesquicentenary 1992* Hobart, Tasmania: Trustees of the Diocese of Hobart, Tasmania.

Taylor, J., D. Wilkinson, and B. Cheers (2006) 'Is it consumer or community participation? Examining the links between 'community' and 'participation'' *Health Sociology Review* 15 (1): 37-47.

Tomlinson, D. (1995) *The Post Evangelical* London: SPCK Triangle.

Tracy, D. (1994) *Plurality and Ambiguity: Hermeneutics, Religion, Hope* Chicago: University of Chicago Press.

Vinson, T. (2007) *Dropping off the Edge: the distribution of disadvantage in Australia* Richmond, Victoria: Jesuit Social Services.

Voth, D. (1979) 'Social Action Research in Community Development' in Edward J. Blakely (ed) *Community Development Research: Concepts, Issues, and Strategies* New York: Human Sciences Press: 67-81.

Warner, R.S. (1990) *New Wine in Old Wineskins: Evangelicals and Liberals in a Small-Town Church* Berkeley and Los Angeles, California: University of California Press, Ltd.

Weber, M. (1965) *The Sociology of Religion*, Translated by Ephraim Fischoff, Introduction by Talcott Parsons, London: Methuen & Co Ltd.

Weber, M. (1976) *The Protestant Ethic and the Spirit of Capitalism*, Translated by Talcott Parsons, Introduction by Anthony Giddens, London: George Allen & Unwin Ltd.

Wierenga, A. (2001) *Making a Life* Unpublished Doctor of Philosophy Thesis, School of Sociology and Social Work, Hobart: University of Tasmania.

Wuthnow, R., J. Hunter, A. Bergesen and E. Kurzweil (1984) 'The phenomenology of Peter L. Berger' in R. Wuthnow, J. Hunter, A. Bergesen and E. Kurzweil *Cultural Analysis: The work of Peter L. Berger, Mary Douglas, Michel Foucault, and Jurgen Habermas* London: Routledge & Kegan Paul: 21-76.

Zijderveld, A.C. (1986) 'The challenges of modernity' in J. Hunter and S. Ainlay (eds) *Making Sense of Modern Times: Peter L. Berger and the Vision of Interpretive Sociology* London: Routledge & Kegan Paul: 57-75.

Appendix 1: Methdological considerations

This book is based on Rev James Collins' doctoral thesis, commenced in 2003 and completed in 2010. The long process of interviewing parishioners from the four communities of faith and transcribing the interviews began in 2005. Professor Douglas Ezzy was his supervisor, and Helen Collins is James' wife. Douglas and Helen have made a 'substantial contribution' to the rewriting of the thesis into the form of a book that justifies their co-authorship.

The research received the approval and support of the Anglican Bishop of Tasmania, John Harrower, and also the approval and support of the Diocesan Mission Enabler (now known as the Director of Ministry Support). Furthermore, the Diocesan Ministry Council, which, amongst other things, is the body elected by the Anglican Diocesan Synod to "Provide for the on-going formation of clergy" (Anglican Church of Australia, Diocese of Tasmania, Ministry Council Ordinance 1999 [Amended 2000]), approved the study at their meeting in February, 2003.

Rev Collins wrote to each Parish requesting that he be given permission to undertake this research. After he received approval from each Parish Council he then asked that the 'Notice for Inclusion in the Parish Newsletter' (see Appendix 4) be included in the weekly Parish Newsletter so that everyone was aware of what was happening and, hopefully, that people would agree to be interviewed. All people who agreed to be interviewed were required to sign a 'Consent Form'. The Human Research Ethics Committee (Tasmania) Network stipulated that people were to volunteer to be interviewed and that Rev Collins was not to recruit people to be interviewed by asking them himself. This project received ethical approval from the Human Research Ethics Committee (Tasmania) Network on the 10th December, 2004.

The fieldwork component of the research comprised the interviewing of people from the four communities of faith of New Norfolk, Channel/Cygnet, St Helens (now known as Break O'Day), and Hamilton. Rev Collins completed a total of 31 interviews: of these, 30 interviews were of parishioners and one interview was of someone outside the parishes who was able to give a Diocesan perspective. This process of interviewing, transcribing, analysis of the data, writing and the on-going iterative process of the re-examination of the interviews, analysis of the data and writing took many years.

'Telling the story' forms a large part of ethnography (Ellis 1997). Part of this story telling might also include one's own story (that is, auto-ethnography). Using auto-ethnography allows for some analysis within the research of Rev James Collins role as an Enabler within the four parishes. This forms only a small, but essential, part of the overall study. Aspects about the role of being an Enabler are incorporated into the four chapters on the four communities of faith.

While primarily ethnographic, because of Rev Collins' position as Enabler in the four communities of faith, the research is also an example of participatory action research. Participatory action research involves a dialectic relationship between understanding (that is, description and analysis) and policy/action. Dick (1995: 2) refers to action research as comprising two aspects: research "to increase understanding" and action "to bring about change". In addition, Voth (1979) makes the point that such research should be a joint effort and the topic being researched should arise out of the community rather than from the person engaged in the research. In framing this research about these four communities of faith, an extended conversation took place between the four parishes, the Diocese, and Rev Collins in consultation with Douglas Ezzy at the University of Tasmania in terms of telling this story, reflecting on it, and sharing it with others. As this conversation unfolded over time during the early part of Rev Collins' candidature this research project 'took shape' into its present form as a dialectical process.

This research had close scrutiny from the University of Tasmania's Human Research Ethics Committee (Tasmania) Network. Entering into the lived experience of the 'other' is complicated in this research given that, as mentioned above, whilst Rev Collins belonged to each of these four rural Anglican communities of faith, he was not a live-in member of any of the four communities. His role as a researcher and as an Enabler (Priest) placed him in an ambiguous position.

In order to make a clear distinction between his work and his research Rev Collins only used what interviewees said in their interview in the research. Nothing that interviewees said outside of the interviews is used in the research. Therefore, if in an interview it became evident that an interviewee was in need of pastoral care it was, in this situation, appropriate to stop the interview, engage in the pastoral situation and then, if appropriate, re-engage with the interview (if the interviewee felt that they were able to continue). All of this was dealt with in an up-front, negotiated way so that the interviewee felt that they were safe and were given the opportunity to decide whether to continue with the interview or not.

In terms of the ethical implications, Rev Collins is perceived to be in a position of power in each of these four rural Anglican communities of faith (the reality is that as an Enabler he enjoys no privileges of tenure or even incumbency). Therefore, he needed to be very conscious of whether people whom he interviewed were telling him what they thought he wanted them to tell me; or, on the other hand, were people not telling him things because of his position? Rev Collins has worked very hard at allowing for honesty within the affairs of the four parishes so that difficult issues can be named and dealt with in healthy and constructive ways, and he hopes that this applies as much to the interviews and to the research. Namely, that people were honest.

Another ethical concern is not so much Rev Collins relationship with the four parishes but his relationship with the Diocese in general and with the Bishop in particular. As a priest, Rev Collins is licensed by the Bishop to whom he is answerable. In the traditional understanding, any priest is under the 'orders' of the Bishop; that is, all clergy in a diocese swear an oath to obey the Bishop "in all things lawful" (wording from the Oaths and Declarations made prior to licensing for a particular priestly role). So, whilst some people within the parishes might look on Rev Collins as having power, he is, in fact, quite powerless in an institutional sense. This adds another level of ambiguity to his role as a researcher and as an Enabler (Priest).

This ambiguity is further heightened by the critique developed within this research regarding the preferred 'style' of being church (namely, the 'success' oriented church-growth model) within this Diocese. This model manifests in some parishes (particularly in the larger urban ones) within the Diocese and appears to be unsuited to the needs of all the parishes (particularly in the smaller rural and urban ones) in the Diocese. The reason for this is it seeks to import a model that, because of demographic, cultural, social and philosophical trends at the local, national and international level, is not applicable in every situation. In addition, within such a 'success' oriented purpose-driven church model there is little analysis or recognition of the social and cultural trends that have brought about profound changes in society. These changes have also strongly impacted on the Diocese, in which there is both a lack of sociological analysis and a persistent hope that someone or something (a model/plan/scheme/programme) will reinvent the Diocese and save it from further numerical and financial decline.

In such a context, the model of Enabler Supported Ministry is quite anarchic as it is a 'ground-up' way of being church that is grounded in the realities of the demographic, cultural, social, and philosophical trends that are evident from the local level to the international level. At the same time, however, ESM is also deeply grounded in theology and church practice. So, it is anarchic from within, while mindful of the riches that come from within and the reality of the effects of the 'outside' world. Geertz (1973: 5) emphasises both the search for meaning in culture and in the research of that culture:

> The concept of culture I espouse ... is essentially a semiotic one. Believing, with Max Weber, that man [sic] is an animal suspended in webs of significance he himself has spun, I take culture to be those webs, and the analysis of it to be therefore not an experimental science in search of law but an interpretive one in search of meaning.

Following Geertz (1973), we have sought to explicate and interpret the meanings that the parishioners attach to their lives, behaviours, and actions in the living out of a new way of being church (ESM). Not only do we describe the meanings that the parishioners attach to their lives of faith, we also seek to understand and interpret them.

One further ambiguity is the relationship between the 'academy' and the Church. We seek to tell the story of these four rural Anglican communities of faith in a sociologically sophisticated way that takes into account the social and cultural context affecting all levels of our society. We also do this in a theologically relevant way. In taking this approach, we are combining the sociological and the theological. In doing this, we are running counter to the trends in the 'academy' where, as Carroll maintains (2008), mainstream Christianity is seen either as irrelevant to the above-mentioned trends (as it has largely been by trying to pretend that they do not exist) or is seen as having lost the capacity to engage any longer in these issues (for the very same reason that it has tried to pretend that it is the sole bearer of truth and that the post-modern world, where pluralism prevails, is not relevant).

We are seeking to convey the 'truth' of these four rural Anglican communities of faith as they engage with their social context. However, we are not seeking to present these parishes as being custodians of the 'only' truth. They represent *a* response to the complex changes in our society and not the *only* response. This research has sought to provide some interpretation of the responses made by each of these four rural Anglican parishes; that is, our interpretation.

Appendix 2: Frequently Asked Questions: Enabler Supported Ministry

Some parishes within the Diocese of Tasmania have moved or are moving to a different model of ministry from the traditional one centred around one rector per parish. This model, which is finding increasing application outside this Diocese and overseas, is known locally as Enabler Supported Ministry, formerly known as Total Ministry. Some of the frequently asked questions about this way of being church, and brief answers, are set out below.

1. What is Enabler Supported Ministry?

Enabler Supported Ministry (ESM) is a model of church where local people are called to form a leadership team, which then takes responsibility for carrying forward the mission of the parish supported by an Enabler. Enabler Supported Ministry is known in other dioceses as total ministry, mutual ministry, common ministry, local collaborative ministry, every member ministry, ministry of the baptized and ministering community.

2. Is ESM Anglican?

Anglican order and ethos, including the three-fold order of bishops, priests and deacons, remain fundamental to the model. It is to be found in a wide variety of Anglican dioceses and traditions.

3. Which Parishes in Tasmania are developing ESM?

To date, nine parishes have adopted Enabler Supported Ministry. These are Break O'Day, Brighton, Channel/Cygnet, Circular Head, New Norfolk, Penguin, Riverlinks, Sheffield and West Coast. Exploration began in 1998. All nine parishes, in conjunction with the Diocese, have called a Local Ministry Support Team and identified those called to serve as Ordained Team Members (OTM). The first ordinations took place in August 2001 and the parishes were Commissioned in February 2002.

4. Has it been approved by the Diocese and does the Bishop support it?

Enabler Supported Ministry has its origins in the Restructuring and Viability Report 1997 and is enthusiastically supported by Bishop John Harrower. The Synod of the Diocese of Tasmania passed an amendment to the Parish Administration Ordinance in 2002 to allow for Enabler Supported Ministry. The Diocesan Bishop and the Ministry Council provide oversight through the Director of Ministry.

5. Who is the leader in an ESM Parish?

In the Anglican Church, the diocese is the primary unit of interdependence and the Bishop is the identifiable leader of all parishes. The leadership model being encouraged and developed in Enabler Supported Ministry is that of Jesus who did not take total control of all ministry, but who modelled ministry and trained and enabled people and sent them out to empower others. St Paul encouraged local leadership in the churches in Asia Minor which was corporate and based on the gifts of the Holy Spirit. Such communities were interdependent, not solely dependent on the input of one single strong leader.

6. What is a Local Ministry Support Team?

A Local Ministry Support Team (LMST/the Team) is a group of baptized people identified and called by the local church to lead them in Enabler Supported Ministry. The Team is made up of people with spiritual maturity and gifts of leadership. The Team does not undertake all of the ministry. Rather it encourages and enables all members to discover and use their own particular gifts for ministry in the life and mission of the church.

7. What is an Ordained Team Member (OTM)?

An OTM is a member of the Local Ministry Support Team who is ordained deacon or priest. All OTM's exercise their ministry as part of the Team. Enabler Supported Ministry parishes are encouraged to call at least two people to serve as OTM's.

8. What is the difference between an OTM and other priests?

OTM's are priests in the Church of God. However, they function as priests solely within the parish in which they serve. Unlike Stipendiary and Honorary Priests they cannot serve in another parish without invitation. If an OTM moves from an Enabler Supported Ministry parish to live in a traditional parish setting s/he will not automatically be able to exercise ministry as a priest. It will be necessary for them to be called to serve as an Honorary Priest in the new context.

9. How are people trained for their roles in an ESM Parish?

Study takes place within the parish in a learning community. Studies in theology and ministry are undertaken by the Local Ministry Support Team and are open to anyone who wishes to participate. Study focuses on everyday life experiences and issues that arise in the life, mission and ministry of the church. The study program is on-going and includes a range of courses and resources.

10. What is an Enabler?

An Enabler is a clergy-person (usually stipendiary) appointed by the Bishop to be a companion to a parish (or group of parishes) as it develops this way of being church. Regular visits to the parish to encourage, train, mentor and evaluate their mission and ministry are part of the Enabler's role.

11. Is an Enabler needed for the long term?

The Enabler is a permanent part of this way of being church. In addition to the role above, he or she provides a link with the diocese and with other parishes.

12. Will standards be lowered if local people lead and do the ministry themselves?

The quality of education and training for ministry undertaken by people in these parishes is of a high standard. The mentor model used is intensive and extends over a number of years. Much of the Biblical and theological reflection that is part of the training program is related to life experiences in the local context. The standard of ministry, as always, depends upon the commitment to growth and the selfless service of godly people for whom we are enjoined to pray regularly.

13. What is the relationship between the Team and the PC?

The Team is not a replacement for the Parish Council or Churchwardens but works in partnership with them in the same way that a rector would. The Team is responsible for the worship, mission and ministry of the parish. The Parish Council and Churchwardens have primary responsibility for the parish finances and fabric, and for all policy decisions and appointments. If the Team wishes to carry out any special initiative it must first gain the agreement of the Parish Council.

14. Is there a solid theological foundation for ESM?

Enabler Supported Ministry understands the Church to be a community of Christians upon which God's grace is lavished in the form of many gifts. The gifts are given to build up the whole body of Christ and to reach out to the local community. Every parish is responsible for recognizing the spiritual gifts and needs of its members, and calling forth these ministries. The Holy Spirit will give to the Christian community members who are gifted for ordained ministry and whose calling and gifting will be discerned through that same Spirit, by the local Christians and diocese.

Appendix 3: Glossary (in the words of the interviewees)

Enabler Supported Ministry (ESM):

Enabler Supported Ministry is a ministry which encourages participation ... by all parishioners or as many as possible. It encourages people to discover and use their gifts within the church. It probably does away with the traditional hierarchy in that all gifts are acknowledged as being equally valuable and some people aren't valued more than others. Of course, it is supported by an Enabler who is a person who isn't a parishioner, but a person who has the necessary experience, qualifications and personality to act as an Enabler within the parish and also to be a link between the parish and the Diocese. (Jane, artist)

I believe it's an accountable form of ministry where the Anglican Church and Anglican ethos can be worked out at a local level with the sacramental ministries being attended to and the pastoral ministries being attended to. So it's a very broad range of ministry that is structured; [it] doesn't just happen in an ad hoc manner. (Graham, business proprietor)

The local church manifesting the gifts of the individual people in the church. I don't think that the Ministry Team could operate and grow and be sustainable without the loving prayerful support of the community here in this parish. And I feel they've got that, totally. (Hester, retired)

Local Ministry Support Team (LMST):

In the context of Enabler Supported Ministry is a Team of people who were called out by the whole parish … as having leadership potential and who agree to undertake a leadership role, [are] prepared to train in that leadership role and to become a member of the Team. The Team itself is a group of people who are there to support the ministry of the congregation and of the parish. They undertake quite a few of those ministries themselves but, essentially, theirs is a coordinating role encouraging other people to take up ministries and supporting them in those ministries. (Mary, writer)

A Team of people is chosen by parishioners to take the place of a permanent resident priest to see to the running of the parish in all facets: administration, the services, and parish pastoral care. (Barbara, retired)

What is the Team? It's presently a group of five people who have the oversight, I guess, co-ordination of all the ministries that would take place in this parish. They're accountable to Parish Council and they jolly well have to learn to work as a team, which I think is great because it doesn't mean that any one person can dominate ... So it's the incumbency: traditional incumbency that's split among the five. (Graham, business proprietor)

The difference for me ... is that the local rector comes and goes; here for three or four years and then gone, where the Local Ministry Support Team is here for ever and a day or until you resign or something like that.... I don't think you can expect one person, especially these days, to have gifts in every area.... With this Local Ministry Support Team you've got people who have got gifts in those areas and they are the experts, more or less. (Tom, retired)

A Calling Out:

A Calling Out in some ways is a little bit like an election except that people aren't invited beforehand to nominate for various roles and parishioners are not given a list of names [of people] to vote for.... There is a period of prayer and discernment before the Calling Out where a specification, a description of the particular role that's being sought is circulated throughout the Parish so that all parishioners have an opportunity to reflect on the kind of person that's going to be needed for this role. They're given time; several weeks to reflect on it and pray about it and discuss it between themselves, if they want to. Then when the actual Calling Out takes place, which is usually after a Sunday morning service, people are invited to write the name or names of people who they feel are called or suitable for that role. It's really then, I think, a matter of the person who comes out clearly as being most widely called is approached by the Enabler to ask if they too feel that calling and if they're willing to accept the role. (Jane, artist)

Local Ministry Support Team's relationship with the Parish Council:

Well ... I think the Ministry Support Team is a team of people who are there to support and encourage, to oversee liturgy, worship, outreach and those aspects of the everyday life of a parish, whereas ... I think the Parish Council is more ... a traditional role. I think people have had more experience of Parish Council than they have of a Ministry Support Team. So, I guess the Parish Council still has the role they always have had, of Wardens and ... the more business administration side of the church. Although, having said that, we do have an administrator on the support Team. (Mary, writer)

Well, the Parish Council, they are property and finance. The Local Ministry Support Team looks after the ministry and mission of the church…. They actually meet together so there's a bit of overlapping there, in amongst the people, but basically the Parish Council look after the finances, all of those things. And they also have their say in the mission of the church, of course. (Pat, florist)

Parish Council:

Parish Council are responsible for the property and the finances of the church. (Pat, florist)

Wardens:

The Wardens are basically responsible for that as well ["for the property and the finances of the church."]. I guess they are the end of the line as far as that goes. (Pat, florist)

Enabler:

[I]t's good that we do have an Enabler because ... we're not just focused on ourselves. There is someone outside of us who just comes in and I would imagine, not being a Team member … just someone else coming in and giving that extra boost and supporting help. (Jenny, retired)

I would find it hard to imagine the whole set-up being as efficient and as able to grow as it is without an Enabler. I think it gives stability. I think it gives a sense of encouragement … to Graham and_Tom, especially in the priestly roles…. I think the Enabler is a presence to the whole Parish…. The Sunday that the Enabler is in the Parish … is a special Sunday. It's taking them back to their roots in the church, in the wider church. (Hester, retired)

Well, as far as your teaching and instruction to the Ministry Team … I can see the proofs of what the Enabler has done and achieved. I know both of the Ministers, the Enabling Team Ministers, have improved and changed considerably in their outlook. It's probably a terrible expression but they've gone from "I'm holier than thou", … to "We are one of you and we're nothing better than you and we're trying to improve our understanding and knowledge of Christianity and impart it to you". That's how I see it. (Ian, retired)

Appendix 4: Enabler Supported Ministry Handbook

Each Christian community shares with the Bishop the responsibility for worship, ministry and mission.

The Holy Spirit calls every Christian into a Christian community.

The Holy Spirit gives gifts for service to every Christian.

Every Christian community has sufficient gifts to carry out its worship, ministry and mission.

Enabler Supported Ministry is a way of structuring ministry so that the local Church is responsible for establishing priorities for mission and ministry

helps us recognize: Every congregation **is** a ministering community, rather than a community gathered around a minister

Every member is a minister

helps us recognize that all Christians have gifts [1 Corinthians 12:11; Ephesians 4:7-12]

"It is not a program or a system but a way of being, a culture"
(Bishop Stewart Zabriskie, Nevada Diocese)

How is it Different?

Enabler Supported Ministry needs commitment to sharing the ministry of the parish.
A Priest is no longer the primary minister in charge.
The main arena for ministry is in daily life.
The Local Ministry Support Team is made up of people from the community of faith.
They are called by the community and licensed by the Bishop.
Some Team members will be lay, some Ordained.

The Role of the Parish Council in Enabler Supported Ministry

In partnership with the Local Ministry Support Team the Parish Council

participates in shaping the mission and ministry of the Parish
keeps in mind the needs of
the local community
the community of faith

shapes policy and is accountable to the Bishop and Diocese for property, finances

ensures that all parish roles are coordinated

accepts responsibility…

for Diocesan policies, practices and standards,

for the regular provision of corporate worship and sacramental ministry

funds ministry costs

The Role of the Local Ministry Support Team

To identify others' gifts

To encourage other members of the Parish into ministry

To organise and support the mission and ministry of the Parish in

Worship, preaching, teaching & reconciliation

Outreach and Evangelism

Pastoral care and social action ministries

Administration

Education and Nurture

The Role of the Enabler

The transition in understanding the role of the enabler must be monitored. It is at this point that many struggle to come to grips with a core element of the model. The Bishop will commission a team of local people to share in the incumbency of the parish taking all roles and responsibilities as defined in the Parish Administration Ordinance. The Enabler is not the rector, rather he or she is a

Companion

Spiritual Director

Coach

Encourager

Supervisor

Troubleshooter

Link with Diocese

Educator and Trainer

Visionary

Storyteller

What differences might we notice?

The Bishop has a key on-going relationship and role with the ministering community in this model:

The clergy will not be in charge

The Local Ministry Support Team may include more than one ordained local minister

Licensed local clergy do not have a seat and vote at Synod

Parish life is not dominated by money raising activity

Key areas of ministry will be supported by a Local Ministry Support Team skilled for this work

The Parish Council has an enhanced role in participating with the whole Parish in decision making about ministry and mission priorities

A much closer relationship with the Diocese

Sacramental Ministry is more readily available on a regular basis

There will be an increase in congregational enthusiasm and participation

Practical support from a ministry Enabler and the Diocesan Mission Enabler

Growth in commitment, faith, membership and mission effectiveness

A strong bond with other ESM Parishes

What are the steps?

The Parish Leadership decide to explore ESM.

The whole Parish completes an educational process.

The Parish decides to adopt Enabler Supported Ministry and an Enabler is appointed.

A Local Ministry Support Team is formed.

The Enabler continues in encouragement, education and training of the Team and Parish.

The Bishop examines the capacity of the team and parish prior to licensing, ordination and commissioning.

The Diocesan Mission Enabler coordinates and oversees the journey.

Stage One: Enquiry

1. A Diocesan Officer is asked to undertake a consultation to include
   Exploration of options for the future
   Financial Concerns
   Teaching about the theology and practice of Enabler Supported Ministry
2. Information about Enabler Supported Ministry is provided to the Parish Council and Wardens.
3. Written request to the Bishop for approval to <u>explore</u> further the model.
4. Proceed to exploration with permission of the Bishop.

Stage Two: Exploration

A Diocesan Officer or the Priest in Charge guides the parish through the following:

Assessment of parish strengths / weaknesses
Identification of mission and ministry priorities
Identification of gifts of ministry for each member
Analysis of financial situation
Leadership potential

Decision to proceed

Parish Meeting and 'ballot' of members
Enabler appointed by the Bishop with Job description and finances agreed
Draft Covenant between Parish & Diocese
Time Frame agreed to commissioning

Stage Three: Calling of the Local Ministry Support Team

Preparing the congregation for calling out process
Calling of people to form the Local Ministry Support Team including identification of those who may be ordained Team members
Interviews - Bishop's Visiting Team for Vocational Advisers
Potential team members approached confidentially
Names affirmed by PC
Ministry Support Team invited to enter into a formation stage by the Bishop
Ministry Support Team presented to the Parish

Commitment to Training Covenant finalised to include:

Personal
Group
General
Draft covenant with Diocese finalised
Interim Local Ministry Support Team formed

Stage Four: Training

During this stage the Parish Enabler works to establish the **Local Ministry Support Team,** the **Parish Council** and the **Parishioners** in the functions of an enabled parish. Understanding the role of an Enabler is crucial during this stage.

Local Ministry Support Team

Individual needs in training
Ministry strengths and passions
Spiritual gifts
Development of Parish Mission Action Plan along with the whole Parish
Working together as the Local Ministry Support Team
Functioning in roles

Parish Council

Define roles and responsibilities

Parishioners

Grow in understanding of ministry gifts
Join ministry/mission working teams

Stage Five: Assessment, Licensing & Ordinations

Review of Progress
Consideration of appropriateness of any Working Agreement
Consideration given to readiness of whole Parish.
Readiness of individuals to take responsibilities as per vision
Members of Bishop's Vocational Advisory Team visit the Parish and make their recommendations to the Bishop assessing readiness for Enabler Supported Ministry
The Bishop considers establishment of the parish as an ESM Parish
A Service of Commissioning to inaugurate Enabler Supported Ministry, Commissioning of the Parish, licensing of the Team and Ordinations

Stage Six: Ongoing Training

Core theological training curriculum continues with at least 2 reviews per annum.
Consideration of the Ministry Support Team development and well-being.
Review/adjustment of ministry licenses.
Consideration of working agreements.
Review development of mission as per ministry priorities.
Pastoral Care
Development of team
Preaching
Development of team
Worship
Development of team
Outreach & evangelism
Administration
Any other Ministry areas
Review Role of Enabler

Second Generation Call

Annual review of Local Ministry Support Team
Learning covenants redrawn for next 12 months.
Search for next generation of ministers
Calling out process activate
Integration of new team members

Review and Possible Exit

This pattern of ministry has demonstrated that constant review works to deliver healthy processes in a parish. A full review of the effectiveness of the model will be conducted in the second year as a commissioned parish with a fully operational team.

Supporting Legislation:
Parish Administration Ordinance 1995
28. Enabler Supported Ministry
(Amended 2002)

Numbers 1-3 will apply where the Bishop has given formal approval for a Parish to consider Enabler Supported Ministry.

Numbers 4-12 will apply where the Bishop has mandated Enabler Supported Ministry if there is conflict with other sections of the Ordinance.

In all other matters the relevant section of the Ordinance will apply.

1. A Parish may decide following the process requirements that follow, to adopt a pattern of ministry organization known as Enabler Supported Ministry.
2. The following procedure shall be followed where parishes wish to consider and/or adopt Enabler Supported Ministry.
    a. Parish representatives shall meet with Diocesan personnel and use resources provided to discover what Enabler Supported Ministry could mean for them.
    b. The Bishop, assisted by the Diocesan Ministry Council, Diocesan Mission Enabler and/or a Diocesan Mission Support Officer, together with the Parish, will assess whether Enabler Supported Ministry is appropriate.
    c. The Parish will hold a properly convened meeting of parishioners at which a vote must determine whether or not the parish will proceed with the Enabler Supported Ministry option.
    d. Final approval shall be given by the Bishop and Diocesan Ministry Council before the process continues.
3. The continuing process for the development of Enabler Supported Ministry in the Parish will include:
    a. The appointment of an Enabler who will be licensed by the Bishop to nurture ministry and Enabler Supported Ministry development.
    b. The worshipping congregation(s) along with the Parish Council will covenant with the Bishop and the Enabler to enter the development of the Enabler Supported Ministry process according to current guidelines.
    c. At an appropriate time, a Local Ministry Support Team (hereafter called "The 'Team") will be called in order to enhance and support the mission and ministry of the whole Parish. In the calling process individuals shall be identified to serve as Ordained Local Ministers.
    d. Following a period of formation, which will include prayer and

study, the Parish and Team shall be commissioned for Enabler Supported Ministry. The service shall include ordination of those called to serve as Ordained Local Ministers. Team members will be licensed for ministry in the Parish.

e. A written Covenant shall be drawn up between the Parish and the Bishop outlining the terms and conditions under which Enabler Supported Ministry will be developed in the Parish and signed by the Churchwardens, members of the Team and the Bishop.

4. In Enabler Supported Ministry Parishes there shall be a Local Ministry Support Team (referred to as 'the Team')

   a. Membership of the Team shall consist of a Coordinator of Administration and other licensed ministers, priests and deacons as agreed and called by the Parish and the Diocese. Other licensed lay ministers may be called, but need not be members of the Team.

   b. The Executive of the Parish Council shall consist of:-

   The Lay Chairperson
   The Wardens
   The Coordinator of Administration
   An Ordained Local Minister elected at the Annual Meeting.

   The Executive of the Parish Council shall administer the day-to-day affairs of the parish in between meetings of the Council. The Executive shall report to the Council, at each meeting, its activities and decisions during the period between the last meeting of the Council.

5. The Local Ministry Support Team shall: -

   a. promote and participate in the mission of the Church and ensure that it is advanced through the parish, by generally seeking the coming of the Kingdom of God.

   b. be responsible for the ordering and conduct of services of worship in the parish.

   c. support and encourage ministry of all baptized members.

   d. support and encourage each other as members of the Team.

   e. meet with the Enabler regularly as a Team and individually as required.

f. report to the Parish Council on mission and ministry matters and make recommendations concerning the same

g. report to the Parish Annual Meeting

6. The role of the Ordained members of the Team shall include:
   a. partnership in ministry with the Team and Parish community.
   b. serving within the community which called them for ordination, as licensed by the Bishop, and shall only function in another parish with the support of the Team and Enabler.
   c. serving in a voluntary capacity
   d. not being eligible to be a Churchwarden
   e. the License ceasing upon movement to another parish or diocese.
7. Unless elected or appointed under any special provisions of Ordinances of the Diocese, those ordained for such local ministry shall not by virtue of ordination be entitled to a seat on Synod. However, the Parish shall elect one of those ordained for such local ministry to be its licensed clergy representative of Synod with both a seat and vote in the House of Clergy.
8. Members of the Team are eligible to receive from the Parish reimbursement for expenses including travel at rates approved by the Diocese from time to time, as agreed by the Parish Council.
9. No more than two members of the Local Ministry Support Team shall be elected to serve as members of the Parish Council. The Coordinator of Administration shall be an ex-officio member of the Parish Council with full voting rights.
10. The primary responsibilities of the Enabler shall include assisting the Team and Parish in:
    a. the development of a mission strategy and encouragement of outreach.
    b. the development of appropriate styles of local ministry.
    c. the ongoing identification of ministry skills.
    d. the facilitation of training programs.
    e. the supervision and mentoring of individuals in the development of their particular ministries.

f. Sunday worship as appropriate.

11.a The Annual Meeting shall determine the number who shall be members of the Parish Council.

b. There shall be no more than three Church Wardens, one of whom shall be appointed by the Team and the Enabler.

c. The number of other members of the Parish Council shall be at least equal to the number of Wardens.

d. For the purpose of any Canon, Ordinance, resolution or rule of Synod the Churchwardens shall be understood to be the Churchwardens of any church building in a parish and of the parish as a whole.

e. The Parish Council shall elect from any member of the Council a person to be the Chairperson and a person to be the Vice Chairperson

f. The Chairperson shall have a deliberate vote only, except in the case of equal voting at an election when the Chairperson shall have a second or casting vote.

g. In case of sickness, accident or death of the Enabler, the Churchwardens shall liaise with the Diocesan Mission Support Officer and/or the Diocesan Mission Enabler.

h. The appointment of an Enabler shall be made by the Bishop in partnership with the Ministry Council, Diocesan Mission Enabler and/or the Mission Support Officer in discussion with the Parish (es) that the Enabler will serve.

12. Enabler Supported Ministry Parishes shall follow all Guidelines published by the Diocesan Ministry Council that pertain to the development of Enabler Supported Ministry. All such Guidelines shall first be ratified by the Bishop and Diocesan Council before coming into force.